Praise f
Development I

"I know I'll make Melanie's b
tices... This book could not have come at a better time for me,
and I recommend it to any psychic who feels a little discouraged
at any stage in his or her advanced development."

—Dr. Alexandra Chauran, author of
365 Ways to Develop Your Psychic Ability

"Between these covers is everything you need to up your psychic
game, right into a professional seat, should you so desire... Why
not employ ALL of your psychic intelligence? Barnum can show
you exactly how to do that, with a lot of fun along the way."

—Cyndi Dale, bestselling author of
Awaken Clairvoyant Energy

"Melanie Barnum's *Psychic Development Beyond Beginners* explores
her personal journey as she opened up to her psychic and mediumship abilities... She explains how to connect with energy,
explore meditation, work through blocks coming from ego, and
how to communicate with spirit guides."

—Kala Ambrose, Your Travel Guide to the
Other Side and award-winning
author of *The Awakened Psychic*

"I really enjoyed the easy flow of the writing in this book. Nothing
was convoluted or hard to understand in Melanie's descriptions
of the many exercises she offers... This is a well-written book that

is simply chock-full of information for the novice and experienced alike. I believe we should always keep growing, and this book will assist in new growth for any medium, beginning or professional."

—Elizabeth Owens, author of *Spirit Messages*

PSYCHIC DEVELOPMENT
BEYOND BEGINNERS

© Bryn G. Mullins

About the Author

Melanie Barnum (Bethel, CT) is an international author of multiple books and the creator of her Psychic Symbols Oracle Cards. She is a psychic, medium, intuitive counselor, life coach, and hypnotist who has been practicing professionally for over twenty years. She was a VIP Reader at Psych Out, a gathering of the nation's foremost psychics, organized by Court TV. Barnum brings comfort and healing through her work with clients, both locally and internationally, and enjoys helping others connect by teaching workshops and seminars.

PSYCHIC
DEVELOPMENT
BEYOND BEGINNERS

Develop a Deeper Understanding
of Your Intuition

MELANIE BARNUM

Llewellyn Publications
Woodbury, Minnesota

First Edition
First Printing, 2019

Book format: Samantha Penn
Cover design: Kevin R. Brown
Editing: Rhiannon Nelson
Project management: Samantha Lu Sherratt

Llewellyn Publications is a registered trademark of Llewellyn Worldwide Ltd.

Library of Congress Cataloging-in-Publication Data
Names: Barnum, Melanie, author.
Title: Psychic development beyond beginners : develop a deeper understanding of your intuition / Melanie Barnum.
Description: Woodbury : Llewellyn Worldwide, Ltd., 2019. | Series: Beyond Beginners Series ; 3 | Includes bibliographical references.
Identifiers: LCCN 2019010431 (print) | LCCN 2019017553 (ebook) | ISBN 9780738760162 (ebook) | ISBN 9780738757179 (alk. paper)
Subjects: LCSH: Psychic ability. | Intuition—Miscellanea.
Classification: LCC BF1031 (ebook) | LCC BF1031 .B263 2019 (print) | DDC 133.8—dc23
LC record available at https://lccn.loc.gov/2019010431

Llewellyn Publications
A Division of Llewellyn Worldwide Ltd.
2143 Wooddale Drive
Woodbury, MN 55125-2989
www.llewellyn.com

Printed in the United States of America

Other Books by Melanie Barnum

The Book of Psychic Symbols: Interpreting Intuitive Messages

*The Steady Way to Greatness: Liberate Your Intuitive
Potential and Manifest Your Heartfelt Desires*

Psychic Abilities for Beginners: Awaken Your Intuitive Senses

*Psychic Vision: Developing Your Clairvoyant
and Remote Viewing Skills*

Llewellyn's Little Book of Psychic Development

Manifest Your Year: Exercises to Make Your Wishes Come True

Psychic Symbols Oracle Cards

This book is dedicated to my mom on the other side.
Now, mom, you have to visit me!
(It looks bad that I'm a medium and
you haven't shown up, yet!)

And to Tom.
Because you love me no matter how
late I stay up to write
… and then some.

And to Molly and Samantha.
I wouldn't be me, without you.

And you, you can be whomever you want.
You need only believe it!

You all deserve nothing but the best!

Contents

Exercises

Acknowledgments

How can I write this book without acknowledging everyone who championed psychic development? I am not the first, and I certainly won't be the last to help get this information into the hands of those who need it most.

All my teachers, the psychics, and authors who have been there for me deserve my gratitude and my utmost respect. The experiences I have shared within the pages of this book would not have been possible without them.

And, speaking of experiences, the people who've shared their stories with you, the readers, deserve a million thanks as well. They bring life and explanation to so many of the chapters. The friends and clients who've shared their stories in many different books, the ones who have stayed on this journey, again, a huge "Thank you!" Thank you for helping so many others grasp what could be their story, their intuition, and their fears.

My sister, who once again, has been there to hold my hand and say, "Just get it on paper. You are amazing!" Thank you, Tammy!

And Adam, for believing in me almost as much as I believe in him, and I do believe that he will be a best-selling author one day!

To my friends and loved ones who encourage and support me with coffee, love, and even the occasional cookies—you know who you are!

And finally, Angela Wix, who, although we've never met in person, seems to know me so well...offering me an extension even though she didn't know I needed an extension! A psychic in her own right, and an amazing editor. Thank you, again!

Most especially, thanks to everyone who chose to read this book! I hope you enjoy it!

Author's Note

The practices and techniques described in this book should not be used as an alternative to professional medical treatment. This book does not attempt to give medical diagnosis, treatment, prescriptions, or suggestions for medication in relation to any human disease, pain, injury, deformity, or physical or mental condition.

The author and publisher of this book are not responsible in any manner whatsoever for any injury that may occur through following the examples contained herein. It is recommended that you consult your physician to obtain a diagnosis for any physical or mental symptoms you may experience.

The stories shared in this book are based on real-life events and readings. Many of the names and some of the circumstances have been changed to preserve privacy.

Introduction

We are all intuitive. But, you know that already. You've gotten this far in life by using your intuition, if only occasionally. You are ready to move on to the next level, to go beyond your beginnings, and tune in to all your psychic gifts. You've likely already absorbed the basics and are looking for more. If not, don't worry! We will cover key basics at the start to ensure we are all moving beyond the beginner phase with a solid foundation in place. Either way, it doesn't matter. It's of no import, because you know, don't you? You know that you've already got something brewing. You've already begun to tap into all the universe has to offer. But, possibly, you're stuck, though you are all set and ready to go. Now is your chance to move to the next level.

Being psychic is natural. It's normal. It's part of your birthright. It is as ordinary as breathing, yet we don't usually treat it that way. It is an innate legacy we have all been bestowed with, though we undoubtedly have not drawn on it nearly as much as we should. Perhaps it doesn't feel as instinctive to you because you've fought against it at some point during your lifetime. Maybe

1

you've discovered that you really are psychic or at the very least, intuitive. Either way, you are at the point when you are prepared to go deeper, to understand more fully what it means to be psychic or to utilize your inherent psychic abilities.

Have you ever felt a sometimes strong or other times gentle nudging that you were missing something? It feels like you should do something, but you can't quite figure out what that is? I, too, have felt it. It starts to gnaw at you a bit, interfering with your daily routine. It makes you feel like nothing is right and you feel a bit hollow. Perhaps it feels as though you are moving under water. That is a call to action; it is one of the ways your spirit tells you to pay attention to your intuition. On every level, whether you're a beginner or a seasoned expert, this feeling can befall you and will most likely last until you recognize it for what it is.

The acknowledgment that you are ready is your opening. Being past the point of curiosity, your spirit knows what is next—feeding that need to tap into your psychic gifts. It is taking a necessary step to expand upon what you already know to increase your awareness across the board. You've moved past the beginning, the inkling that there was more to life than the naked eye could see, and you have more than just a passing interest in psychic abilities. Circumstance, curiosity, and need have brought you to this new level of alertness. You have already begun to grasp that there is more to reality than the naked eye can see; now it is up to you to become more familiar with how to foster that reality to become part of your everyday world.

By now you've gone through life, possibly feeling unfulfilled or yearning for more. It can feel this way because you've maybe just scratched the surface of your psychic potential. It can feel like you've gotten lost a bit, even though you've already begun tuning in to your intuition. It's okay to feel lost, because you're moving in the right direction. You are reaching beyond where you've already been and are feeling the physical and organic pull toward your psychic abilities. Chances are, because you've decided to explore your gifts further, you've discovered you are very intuitive. You are already psychic, and you're lucky enough to realize it. You've detected the psychic vibrations that are with you and around you and are ready to decipher them with your abilities. This joy of making sense out of the energy around you is what's been on the edge of your consciousness, distracting you and drawing you out—making you feel as though there was something you weren't quite grasping.

Take your time, now. Enjoy the process of developing your intuitive gifts further. Have trust in the process and don't try to rush it. If you force your development, whether you are a beginner or an expert, it will create friction and won't feel right, like sucking too hard on a straw and pinching it shut. Being patient and building a strong foundation to work from will allow you to progress further. As much as we all want to instantly utilize every bit of our abilities, it doesn't typically happen without some cultivation. We can expand our knowledge by connecting with our own soul and bringing to the surface what we possess but we may not have nurtured in full, yet.

Don't forget how much you've already learned! You've come a long way and you've gone through a lot discovering your intuitive gifts. Respect your psychic intelligence (the knowledge and natural perception you've developed of the power to bring in a greater extrasensory understanding) and the wisdom you've attained.

Regardless of where you feel you are, you can sit easy knowing you are exceptional and capable of bringing even more to your world. Carry everything you've studied and practiced forward but do it with an open mind. You want to leave room to learn more and be open to a different way of accessing your psychic abilities than you may have learned before. Don't close yourself off because you feel vulnerable, or because you feel you've already been there, done that. Loving the learning process is what will help propel you to the next stage in your development. Now is the time to answer your higher calling. You're taking your first step into a larger world.

At the beginning of every phase of psychic development you have a choice whether to keep going beyond the basics or to halt your progression and rest, giving yourself a chance to digest what you've learned and where you're at in your metaphysical life. The potential to increase your gifts is always there and taking the next step on your journey won't ever reverse what you've already learned. When I do readings for my clients I always tell them what I see psychically based on their greatest potential. I also allow that they will make their own choices and those choices will affect that result. What I am able to share with them, based on what I receive as the best possible outcome, can help guide them in making their own decisions to provide them with an end product they will be happy with. The decisions you make moving forward will continue to add to your knowledge or will provide you with a break from your training. Either way, what you've learned will always be there for you to continue analyzing, and more important, playing with when you are ready.

Where I'm Coming From

We don't always choose who we will be when we grow up. Heck, we usually don't *know* what we want to be, or we change our mind twenty times before we even crest our teen years. Mostly, when we are young, we want to be teachers, doctors, daredevils, firefighters, performers, and parents. Being a psychic is not something we typically aspire to, unless, as a child, you have profound experiences that affect your intuitive senses. The reality is, most of us don't develop a deep understanding of the metaphysical world until we begin studying it, feeding the drive or the need to comprehend the unknown.

I started out as an accountant and was the controller of a company. This career is totally left-brained as it's rational, logical, analytical, and dare I say, kind of boring. (Nothing against accountants!) However, I never felt completely fulfilled. It was like I was missing something, and I felt somewhat hollow. My right brain needed a challenge. That spiritual side, the metaphysical, artistic, intuitive, and creative part of me, needed nourishing. During my tenure as controller, we hired an outside firm to do personality and aptitude assessments for all our department supervisors. They charted our test results and mine looked like a perfect diamond. Turned out I was completely balanced, right- and left-brained, both detail-oriented and holistic, which, according to them, is very unusual. Most people are naturally slanted in one direction or another. This was the beginning of my knowing, validation that there was more to me, and to what I needed, to help make me feel like a complete and whole person.

When I was a teenager, I never knew I would be a professional psychic, hypnotist, and author, and I'm still amazed I get to live in this incredible world, understanding there is more to life than the naked eye can see. When I began my journey, about twenty years ago, I decided I needed to set out to learn as much as I could about psychic abilities. I was born with natural intuition, which I knew, but I was "told" in a message I couldn't ignore that I had to "Do this work now!" It felt like I was hit over the head and I heard those words while standing in my dining room. Being rational and logical, I could not just dive in and change my life or my family's life. I needed to explore and study what it meant to be psychic and what it entailed. That's when I started absorbing everything I possibly could, knowing at that point I would become a working psychic and that I would help others and teach them to tune in to their gifts as well.

Some people grow up talking to dead people and others have a life-changing event or accident that triggers their gifts. Still others, like myself, find themselves suddenly blessed with abilities that can be further developed. Regardless of how it happens, our natural extrasensory perception can be enhanced with practice. When I was metaphysically hit over the head, I knew it was my turn to further develop my intuition, so I started taking classes and studied with more advanced psychics and mediums. During those classes, I found I was doing better than I could have imagined and I knew I'd found my calling—it was no longer something I was told to do, instead it was something I couldn't *not* do.

I offered free sessions to be sure I felt comfortable, but quickly progressed into renting office space and offering my services professionally. I knew I was no longer a beginner, just starting out. I was more advanced, and I needed to share my gifts with others through readings and teaching. I also added many other modalities, including becoming a certified hypnotist and a certified reflexologist and Reiki master. I realized I loved learning and wanted to add other complimentary holistic services to my repertoire.

I also found the more I tuned in, the more I *could* tune in. This has become a more natural state for me and I find myself doing casual, off-the-cuff readings quite a bit. A while back I was with a friend, Patty, working in the snack shed for our high school football team. We started talking and she told me about a medium she had been to see, telling me she was a believer in psychic ability but was always skeptical. She also told me she loved readings. As she spoke, I began experiencing a sense of winter and I could feel snow in the air though it was a warm, early fall day. I immediately got an impression of Patty skiing.

"Do you ski?" I asked her.

She responded with a strange look on her face, "No. I don't."

"Hmm. Who's the M name? I'm getting Michael or Matthew and I see you skiing with a group of friends," I continued, knowing this was important.

"I don't know. I'm not a skier," she continued, still looking very strange.

"I'm sensing this was a long time ago, and I'm now seeing bloody mittens. I feel like something tragic happened and you've never really talked about it since then. I'm sensing a bizarre, tragic accident. Are you sure you didn't ski? I'm getting an M name still, and this young man is here for you," I persisted.

I normally would not have pushed it, but I was well aware of how Patty felt, that she enjoyed and was awed by psychic ability and mediumship. I was also sure this "M" person was coming through for her.

"OH MY GOD! I've never told anyone this story! No one knows, in all my years I have not shared this with anyone! How could you know about this?" she finally confessed.

"All I know is that 'M' is coming through, saying you did all you could and that he appreciates it. Everything is okay, he says, and it's his way of letting you know he's around. Are you going to tell me what happened?" I continued with curiosity.

"Wow. When I was a teenager I went on a class ski trip. I was with a group of girls and a kid from another school came down the mountain and lost control. He crashed into one of the ski lift supports, right next to us. We tried to help him, but he was not doing well. I remember my brand-new wool mittens—looking down at them covered in blood. I can't believe you picked up on that. And, his name was Matthew. I don't know how you knew that. I don't know why he would have come to you for me? It was so long ago. I'm in total shock," she answered, clearly flabbergasted and surprised.

"He's just letting you know he's around and appreciates that you all tried to save him. He knows you watched him go down the mountain. He's also providing the proof you need to believe that I'm connecting to your energy," I told her.

We talked about it some more and both knew Matthew had made a special visit. It was amazing. The fact that Matthew randomly came in to connect to Patty was incredible. But, what was even more incredible came afterward. About a week later Patty texted me.

"So, I never, ever told anyone in my family of the ski accident (my husband knew way back then, but we've never spoken of it in twenty-five years). I also never mentioned last week's thing with you. Lucy, my daughter, woke up this morning and said she had the most vivid dream of her entire life. She said she thought everything was totally real life, not a dream (her words), and as she began to tell me I lost my footing. She explained her dream, but it was MY day and our skiing and the boy and the blood on the mittens and clothes, and how we waited and waited for help. And, how he went in the back of a ski mobile in a toboggan and was wrapped in a blanket and how we were covered in blood and had to go down the mountain and we went back to the lodge and just sat and sat and sat and called the hospital. Holy crap! What's going on? I feel like I could sleep the whole day away, I'm physically, mentally, and emotionally exhausted!"

I told Patty that Matthew was, again, just letting her know he was around. I also heard him tell her, "Thank you, thank you, thank you, thank you." She shared that four thank yous made sense as there were four people there. He had found a doorway in and used it to make Patty aware of his presence and his gratitude. I, too, became aware of Matthew as he had hung around for the past week and popped up during my other sessions. I think he was just happy to find a way to communicate. We, Patty and I, were both happy he had chosen us for that.

I regularly do readings for people all around the world, and I teach individuals and groups through workshops and books to tune in to their own gifts. This is my path and how I progressed from a beginner to a professional.

Where You're Going

Everyone is different. We all have different lives and lifestyles. We participate in different activities than even our best friends every day. We enjoy different foods and different entertainment. Yet, all of you have chosen to go beyond your own beginning. Which begs the questions, why are you reading this book? What are you hoping to get out of it? What can developing your psychic abilities beyond a beginning level do for you? These are questions you, yourself can begin to answer, now.

Chances are, you've discovered you either have a natural talent with psychic abilities or you are extremely curious and want to take it to the next level. Developing your gifts beyond where you've gone before will feel powerful. It is about releasing the hold your physical mind has put on your spiritual self and allowing that part to really blossom. When you have your psychic senses available to you, at your command, everything in life will bloom more beautifully.

Within the pages of this book, you'll find a variety of methods essential to master a multitude of techniques, which will allow you to attain a higher level of confidence in your abilities. Using true stories from my client sessions as well as client feedback and interpretations, you will easily understand the psychic development examples presented to further your own skills. The exercises offered will prepare you for deepening the connections you will create with your metaphysical self. Some people will find it helpful to prerecord the exercises so you can close your eyes and listen to the exercises out loud.

In chapters 1 through 3, you will notice some basic concepts that you may have already worked with. Think of this as your foundation, the jumping-off point that will also contain new or deeper concepts, as well as different ways to get you to where you need to be to go beyond. This is also a good place to discover exactly what you're already familiar with and what you need to work on to prepare you to move to the next level. In chapter 4, we really start to amp up our psychic practices, introducing you to metaphysical concepts and extrasensory experiences. Chapter 5 is where the "beyond beginner" phase really takes hold, acquainting you to many ideas, thoughts, and concepts that will have you thinking of your gifts from a fresh perspective. Get ready to dive in and unleash your power!

Regardless of where you are in your psychic journey, you will reinforce your gifts as you move through the book. You will become better acquainted with the way energy behaves, in your ethereal body as well as with your connection to the universe and to loved ones on the other side. You will learn in chapter 6 that becoming a medium may be an added benefit to expanding your psychic abilities, for yourself and others. Venturing outside of your physical body will take you on a voyage to previous lifetimes and can also bring you to a different location in the present moment, providing you with the opportunity to utilize both trips to enhance and deepen your psychic abilities. Your recognition of symbolic messages will intensify, allowing you to better connect with your own intuition and communicate with the other side in a more evidential way. You may find you develop a profound need to share your gifts with others professionally and in chapter 10 you will learn about many ways to bring that desire to fruition. Overall, you'll find a plethora of information at your fingertips to provide you with a more concentrated awareness to take you beyond a beginning level.

Enjoy Your Journey!

There are many ways to remember your journey throughout this book. One of the best ways is to get a blank journal or notepad. Recording your unique experiences will help you along the way as you develop your own psychic abilities. For every exercise you will have answers or outcomes. Before embarking on each new training, open your journal to a fresh page and have a pen ready to record your observations and responses. Be sure to write down which chapter and exercise number you are journaling about. That way you can always go back and review and compare your original results to any new experiences you choose to repeat. It also gives you a chance to reflect upon how far you've come!

You may have heard that anything worth doing is worth doing well. I take that a step further and submit that you should not move forward with psychic development, on any level, unless it brings you happiness. When you are really good at something you usually enjoy doing it. The same holds true for psychic abilities. If you feel as though you are truly connecting and excelling at tuning in to your gifts, you will be more apt to want to continue. However, enjoying your gifts also means you enjoy the learning process. Know that sometimes you will be better at being able to intuit information than other times. This is perfectly okay! Don't allow possible setbacks and even confusion to take away from your appreciation and the joy it brings you. You may feel self-doubt creeping in along the way as well. This is normal— just shake it off and allow the opportunities to develop your gifts to keep coming. Remember, enjoy the process! If you are *never* having fun when working with your psychic abilities, you really need to take a step back and decide if this is for you. Challenging yourself is good, and healthy on many levels, but it should never feel like a chore.

CHAPTER 1

Back to Basics

To go beyond a beginning level is a deepening of awareness and the gifts you currently have. It's not about secret methods or joining any advanced clubs. And, it's not about using bigger words or a stronger vocabulary to make you feel like it's, in some way, more developed or important. Knowing this, we can all move forward and share our experiences of what it means to go beyond our own personal beginning.

I always tell people that everyone can play a note on a piano, but not everyone will be a Beethoven. It's the same with psychic abilities. All who study will not develop the same or want to use their gifts in the same way. However, it all stems from playing that one note; we must go back to the basics in order to build upon our abilities and advance them beyond a beginning level. It's about growth—moving from a complete novice level to one who is more adept in the metaphysical world. And, it is about working harder (practice), seeking more, and intensifying the basic principles of intuition to expand your metaphysical intelligence.

Before We Go Deeper

There's no special magic or different set of skills needed to deepen your abilities. Taking it back to the basics does not mean starting from the beginning or starting from scratch. It is simply a way of deepening your connections and increasing your potentially limitless psychic gifts. Though there is no magical switch to turn on, practicing will increase your skills. What *is* magical is the way you can advance your understanding of the way it all works—this is your metaphysical intelligence. Gordon Smith, a practicing medium, teacher, and author shares that "no matter how much you think you know, or how far you think you have come on the spiritual path, there is always something to be gained by remembering the beginning of that journey."[1]

There is no formula to use that tells you what degree of psychic ability you possess. As a matter of fact, there really is no measurement to grade you on, there's no steadfast rule to follow. While one person may have a better or deeper connection to the metaphysical world than another, we can never really compare two that may be on the same level. Take, for example, math. You can't jump to advanced calculus before learning how to add 2 + 2, but once you've mastered basic addition, you might excel at geometry where someone else more easily develops their understanding of algebra. You, for instance, may excel at tuning in to a sitter's (client's) past, while your friend may be better at precognition, or intuiting the future.

As with math, however, you need a general understanding of how to connect psychically before you can go deeper. If you are

---

1. Smith, Gordon. *Intuitive Studies: A Complete Course in Mediumship.* London: Hay House UK, 2012.

reading this book you probably have at least some basic intuitive knowledge or a vested interest in connecting to the other side. You will get more out of the exercises and chapters here if you are acquainted with psychic abilities already. While sometimes the exercises may seem rudimentary, it is up to you to go deeper.

Who You Connect With

There are so many ways to connect and receive information through your psychic gifts. You may already be accessing the other side via any number of these, but do you know where your messages are coming from? Many people are unaware of who they are actually "talking" to when they tap into their psychic senses—they just know the information is there. This is perfectly fine, usually. You want to be sure you are not connecting to anything harmful or any entities that may have undesirable intentions. Discovering who is sharing data with you will enable you to broaden your abilities and even expand your gifts.

So often we feel our loved ones around us, so we assume it must be them reaching out. Sometimes it is. But, frequently, it's your guides, or even your angels communicating with you. They have been with you for a long time, probably even lifetimes, to help you. We each, individually, have a multitude of guides, ready and waiting for you to ask them for assistance.

There are some key features to remember about each type of helper. Deceased loved ones have either met you in life, are part of your family, possibly even a few generations removed, or are as close as relatives, like special friends, and so on. Relatives do not have to be blood related to come through as loved ones; they can be in-laws or adopted relatives or even foster care family members.

Spirit guides can be distant relatives you've never met from many generations ago or people that are just here to help you. Unlike spirit guides, angels have never walked the earth.

So, now that you know who everybody is, let's talk about what they can do for you. Deceased loved ones were real people and know a lot about you. Therefore, they have gone through the same types of struggles as well as the same types of joy that you may be experiencing. They also retain many of the characteristics they possessed when they were on this side with us. Because of this, they are the perfect helpers to ask for everyday assistance. However, you need to ask them for help with things they were good at when they were here. For example, I wouldn't ask somebody for help with sports if they were terribly clumsy and never played a sport their entire life. But, I would ask someone who was an athlete for help with athletics. When my mom was alive she was an incredible nurse and healer. But she was terrible with finances. So, I ask her for help with healing all the time, but I make sure to stay clear of asking her for help with money!

Spirit guides are a bit different from deceased loved ones. We have many guides on the other side to help us. We have some general guides that stay with us and can help us with a little bit of everything. And, we have some specific guides that can help with whatever we need. Using the same example of sports, we can ask for an athletic guide to help us when we need to accomplish a goal in a sporting event. We can also ask a book-smart guide to help us pass a test at school. And when we need to have a good time, we can ask for our joy guides to come to us.

Angels help us with the big things, like saving lives. They're there to help you pull your best friend out of a car wreck or to give you the strength to swim back to shore after being drawn out by the tide. They also help nudge you in the right direction to fulfill your soul's purpose. There's a hierarchy of angels starting with the archangels and going down to the basic, everyday angels. In general, archangels have more power and can be in more than one place at the same time, which is different than regular angels.

If you're still not sure who you might be talking to you can ask. Asking who they are might present you with a fuller picture of what they can accomplish for you or what they can help you to accomplish. It also gives you a greater opportunity to utilize their gifts and abilities to communicate messages to you in a way that you can understand.

Defining Your Abilities

Defining what psychic abilities are is essential to every budding and developed psychic. Whether you are a professional or you are simply hoping to increase your innate awareness, it is important that you have a grasp on the multitude of psychic senses available to you. Knowing what each sense can provide you affords you the opportunity to build up your strengths as well as strengthen your weaknesses. Focusing on each sense individually can help you expand your psychic comprehension more fully. We'll go through the basics of each ability here now. The alternative is to fly by the seat of your pants and just hope the information comes to you in a way you can understand, which in some cases will continue to happen.

The Clairs

You can't even think about developing your psychic abilities without diving into your clairs. *Clair* is the French word for clear and we use it to describe each of our psychic senses. Clairvoyance, or psychic vision, is one of the most widely recognized senses and is often confused as having the same meaning as the word *psychic*. Clairvoyance, however, allows you to see images or even the deceased, psychically, in your mind's eye. There are two psychic senses that are similar: clairsentience and clairempathy. Clairsentience is a commonly utilized psychic ability and it is what allows you to feel physical and emotional states and things that are not yours. It is also the psychic sense you use when you have a gut instinct about something. Clairempathy means you feel someone's emotions, like taking on their happiness or sadness. Clairaudience is the ability to hear psychically. When you hear messages in your mind, such as words or music or even sounds, it is your clear hearing you are using. Claircognizance means you just know things for which you have no basis or evidence for knowing. A somewhat universal form of claircognizance is knowing someone is about to call before the phone rings. These are the most common clairs and are a crucial part of developing your abilities deeper. There are a couple more, though. Clairalience is another psychic sense, which is the gift of discerning scent, and clairgustance is when you taste psychically. All of these are psychic senses you might have experienced.

I am often asked which senses I use to connect. For me, I use a combination of all my psychic senses. I let the information come to me in whatever form it's sent and ask for clarity if I don't understand it. I've always felt things about people or places, clairsentiently, believing that everyone else did this as well. And, I've known things, claircognizantly, growing up. As I began developing more, my clairvoyant and clairaudient senses became enhanced. Receiving messages with all available psychic gifts can present you with a bigger picture. The more input you have, the more you can translate it into words. Just like with our five physical senses, having access to more data affords us the opportunity for more accurate communications.

I did a phone reading for a client many years ago. She was a new client I had never spoken with previously. Before every session, I do a quick meditation to tune in to my next client. I write down any impressions I receive, including information I perceive with all my psychic abilities, without censoring the data or qualifying how I get it. This client, Kim, was no different. One of the images I saw was of babies on a cloud. To me, this is symbolic of having lost children, either through miscarriage or abortion or stillbirths. I felt this was unintentional loss and the babies had not made it to term. Kim had miscarried during a couple of pregnancies. I was using both my clairvoyance and my clairsentience to receive this specific information and to clarify exactly what it was I was getting for her.

As the session began, I went over everything I had written down. I told her she had babies on the other side, watching over her.

"I feel like they never made it here on earth, but that they're around you often, available to help you when you ask for it," I continued.

"Wow. That's amazing. That makes me feel better about what's happened," she replied. "But, I have to ask, do you think I'll ever be pregnant again? My doctor said I wouldn't be able to."

She explained she already had children after I told her I saw her with kids, but she told me they were with her ex-husband.

"I would love to have at least one with my current husband," she explained.

I tuned in, allowing all my senses to pick up anything I could share with her and what I got was at first promising, but then felt a bit sad as well, though I wasn't sure why.

"I am getting that you'll be pregnant again, against all odds, and you will be due in June. But, it may not have the expected outcome."

"Okay, wow! Thanks!"

Later, Kim contacted me for another reading. During the reading she told me she had gone to the doctor, the same one who had told her she wouldn't be able to conceive again, and he confirmed she was pregnant with a due date in June. Unfortunately, shortly after, she miscarried again. That explained the sadness I had been getting.

I told Kim of the sadness I had experienced, and I shared that I thought a miscarriage would occur again if she did indeed conceive. I asked her how she was.

"I'm okay with it. At least now I know, and I feel like I don't have to try anymore. I have wonderful kids that I'll focus all my energy on. I'm just shocked that you were able to see that I would be pregnant when my doctor told me there was no way! And, you got the due date of June!"

I felt bad for Kim but was happy she was able to move on. By using many different psychic abilities, I had tuned in to Kim and got some detailed information for her. I used my clairvoyance to see her pregnant, my claircognizance to know June would be the due date, and my clairsentience to feel the sadness around the miscarriage. I used clairempathy to feel her sadness at the loss of the baby as well.

Tuning In

So, how do you tune in? Do you stick to only one or two of your psychic senses? Feeling comfortable with a couple modalities should not stop you from exploring the others. Everyone tends to have a prevalent psychic sense or two. And this is great! But there's more out there for you, and if you're already connecting, this is your chance to go even deeper. It's not just about expanding your senses, it's about developing them. You already have the capability to utilize all your intuitive senses, they just need to be activated.

We have always had psychic abilities—they are part of our birthright. Often, though, they lay dormant within and need to be accessed and spiritually charged to start them up again. Whether you've been shut down as a child and feel like you've lost the association with them, or you have been focused more on some abilities so you don't feel the link to the others, this can be fixed. The best way to reactivate your psychic gifts is to set them in motion by using them. It may feel a bit strange at first, or even take you completely out of your comfort zone; change can be awkward. But, it doesn't have to be difficult. To move forward, to rediscover your gifts that may be on the back burner, you need to discover what your dominant psychic sense is.

EXERCISE
. . . .
What Is Your Dominant Sense?

Before you begin, and with most of the exercises to follow, bring your journal to a place you won't be disturbed. Be sure to go somewhere you can be calm and comfortable.

Discovering your dominate sense can help bring you to your next level of awareness. You may already be conscious of which psychic sense you use most. If so, you might, instead, uncover which sense is your main helper sense.

Begin by taking five deep breaths and close your eyes. Feel your toes relaxing. Take another breath and as you exhale, allow that relaxation to rise upward through your legs, into your hips. On the next long, deep breath, that feeling of total relaxation travels through your abdomen and into your chest. Breath again and allow that same feeling to reach all the way out to your fingertips. One more breath and the relaxation spreads through your neck and your face, loosening your jaw and facial muscles. Let the relaxation move right up to the top of your head.

Now, imagine yourself standing in front of a door. On the other side of the door you'll have access to your psychic abilities. In a moment, you are going to open the door and you will meet your guide, someone who is your helper from the other side. It may be one you've already met or may be someone new.

Before you open the door, set your intention to notice which sense presents your guide to you. On the count of three, with your physical eyes remaining shut, you will open the door. One, take a deep breath. Two, put your hand on the door knob and turn. And, three, open the door and pay attention to how you perceive your guide.

Did you see them? Feel them? Hear them? Smell them? Taste a flavor? Just know who they are? Did you feel their emotions?

Now, take it a step further. Did you experience them first with one sense and then another immediately after? Take note of what you met. Did you receive impressions the way you expected? Or was it different in some way?

Let's keep going. Using your sight, describe in detail what your guide looks like. Using your hearing, listen to what they have to tell you. How do they feel to you, and how do they make you feel? Is there anything you know about them that you didn't immediately? Can you taste anything while standing there? Is there a prevalent scent?

After you've exhausted all your psychic senses, take a couple of deep breaths. When you are ready, open your eyes and immediately write down your impressions in your journal. Which sense did you use first? This is generally your dominant sense. Which did you use second? This is usually a helper sense. Does this fit into your normal practice? Was it surprising?

You did great! This is just the beginning. You can touch back to this exercise and do it again while reading this book to see if your answers vary. You might discover your dominant sense changes with practice.

. . . .

Using all your psychic abilities gives you a broader span with which to work. Don't limit yourself by only utilizing the gifts you feel most comfortable with. When you tune in to do a reading for yourself or someone else, allow the information to come in every way. Focus on each individual sense and see what information presents itself. You may not receive impressions with every sense, but be open to whatever you do get. In our quest for psychic knowledge it is always best to expand our awareness to include each sense we have in our reserve.

Recognizing the Level of Psychic Abilities

Recognizing which psychic ability you are using is not essential, but when you are accessing your gifts, it is a critical step to develop your intuition in the beginning. This is because understanding which abilities you use helps ensure you are not just tapping into your imagination.

Ascertaining which gifts you employ when you try to tune in is only important when you are trying to practice and develop those particular skills. When you are at a level that you sense things without worrying about what specific ability you are using, most likely you are beyond a beginning level. Knowing exactly how you're getting the information becomes less important. Think of it in terms of driving a car; when you are a brand-new driver, you need to know how to do everything, like where to put your hands on the wheel and how hard to press the gas, and so on. But, after you've driven for a while it becomes natural, and you don't think about it, you just do it. It becomes automatic, much like the more you practice using your psychic gifts, the more natural it will feel, and you won't have to dissect how it works.

Release the Fear

There are two very different paths to living, whether it's in the metaphysical or the physical realm. One is very easy and the other is more difficult. Author and spiritual teacher Marianne Williamson states, "Our deepest fear is not that we are inadequate. Our deepest fear is that we are powerful beyond measure. It is our light, not our darkness, that most frightens us."[2] Being afraid to come into your power can hold you back.

Coming to a place where you are comfortable using your psychic gifts can be a scary path for many. Acting in fear and trying to increase your grasp on your abilities is a study in futility. Fear does not allow positive energy to come to you. It actually blocks positive energy. Love, however, opens you to receiving goodness. It creates a positive space to expand your power and bring a higher level of fulfillment. But, it can be extremely hard to let go of the fear that holds you back. We tend to be conditioned to be afraid of anything we believe we can't control. When we don't have total control of our intuitive gifts, it can cause confusion, which can lead to fear.

I have been a professional psychic for almost twenty years, doing one-on-one readings. But, I also love to be up on stage, teaching others and giving messages from deceased loved ones. This combination is what truly energizes me and even gives me a rush. The problem with doing this is I have let fear hold me back on many occasions. It is not fear of not being good enough, per se; it is more the fear that nothing and no one will come through for

---

2. Williamson, Marianne. *A Return to Love: Reflections on the Principles of A Course in Miracles.* New York: Harper Collins Publishers, 1992.

me to connect me to my audience. After all, we can't demand the dead talk to us, right?

Stage Fright

Many, many years ago, I was sitting in the front row of a nighttime show at Omega, a holistic learning institute in Rhinebeck, New York. I had been attending a weeklong workshop and had done a good job at not sharing that I was already a practicing psychic. (I've found telling people tends to change the dynamic with the other students and I was there because I enjoy learning and contributing like the others present.) But, on this night, the last night, our teacher John Holland, a respected psychic medium, was putting on a medium demonstration. He came on stage and opened the show by explaining what he would be doing and told us a few funny anecdotes, part of his process. He then told us he would leave the stage and be back in a little bit to start readings, again, part of his process.

John went into a back room somewhere and my fellow students and I began a conversation. We talked about what brought us there and if we were having a good time. I was very comfortable with the two people I was sitting between. They were a mother and daughter duo and we had worked together a bit during the week. They told me they thought I had done really well during the week and was very good at tuning in. I informed them then that I was indeed a professional psychic. They said in tandem, "Well, that explains it!"

They asked me what I wanted to do. I replied, "This. This is what I want to do. I want to teach to large groups. I want to read for large audiences."

Of course, the next thing they asked was, "Then, why don't you? You're good enough!"

It was hard for me to explain the fear that held me back. As I said, it wasn't a fear of being on stage in front of people. I had done that often enough already. Putting myself out there, to do readings when I had to depend on the messages coming through was what scared me. Counting on dead people to talk to you can be unnerving when you are in front of hundreds of people who are waiting with bated breath to see if their loved ones are going to come through.

"Okay, but, why wouldn't they?" they asked. "The deceased want to use you to help them. Of course they will come through. You've already proven you can understand them."

Again, hearing their words did not quell my anxiety of actually doing it—being on stage at the mercy of the deceased.

"I know that's the logical way of thinking, but none of this is logical. It doesn't work that way. Putting myself out there…it just causes my heart to race!" I told them with a chuckle, a bit self-consciously.

It was at that moment that John Holland came back out. He began walking up the stairs to the stage. As he did, he started telling the audience he always has a moment of alarm, worrying that nothing will come through. Then he told us, "But, in this line of work, you have to trust that the other side wants to communicate and will use us as much as possible."

That was awesome. He had the same fears as me. But what was really incredible was the next part. He stopped, mid-stair, turned, and looked right at me. In an audience of hundreds, he pointed to me.

"I trust they will always come through and so should you!" and he continued up the stairs to the stage, leaving me and my two friends with our jaws on the floor.

Don't Be Afraid

Aside from worrying whether a spirit from the other side will come through, one of the greatest fears for a budding psychic is whether or not they can trust their reading as being accurate. Sharing the messages we receive is a daunting task if we're not sure of what we are getting, or we doubt the legitimacy of the missive. Needing to be right, or the desire to only give information that can be immediately validated, can create incredible angst when trying to divine messages for someone. The fear that we are wrong or that it's only our imagination is a rational concern. Holding back what comes through can actually hinder your session but, often, it is hard to trust the information is genuine.

We don't want to be wrong. Yet, we don't give ourselves the opportunity to be right if we don't honestly share the psychic impressions we get. I tell people all the time, "Give what you get!" Don't discount the information you sense. What may seem irrational or ridiculous to you can mean everything to the person you are reading for, and usually does. Get over yourself! It's not about you. Stop holding back because you are afraid to be incorrect. Take the chance you may be right. And, you know what? You may be wrong sometimes, too, but that's okay.

Our own fears hold us back. Yes, it is true that we must have an affinity for the work, or at least a deep understanding of how to connect to our intuition, but we must trust the process. Being afraid of anything in life will cause us to not be able to move forward. Taking the leap of faith and trusting the information you share is what you are authentically intuiting is what will separate you from the other intuitives who hold back.

Going Back Again

No matter how much you already know, you've likely discovered something about yourself in this first chapter. Whether it's learning which is your dominant psychic sense or it's learning who the communications come from, going back to the basics has recharged your psychic batteries and presented you with a different way to think about your gifts. This is also a great time to look at how you feel about those abilities. Acknowledging that you probably have some fears holding you back is a good way to address those fears. Working through the exercises, and even repeating them, can provide you with a higher level of understanding and, in turn, warrant greater confidence in your gifts. By taking it back to the basics, you've prepared yourself for extending beyond the beginning and laid the foundation for understanding symbols and signs.

....

CHAPTER 2

Psychic Symbols and Psychic Representations

We acquire sensory impressions through our five senses every day. From people to situations to emotions, we pick up on visual and audio signals that help us interpret our surroundings. These we often refer to as social cues. We are able to detect the subtle indicators that we can then react or interact with. We learn to recognize these through our exposure to them. Psychic messages work in much the same way. We can psychically pick up symbolic information, which prompts us to translate the data and before you know it, you're interpreting psychic messages.

Psychic Symbols

To get an accurate picture of what I share with my clients, I rely on all my gifts, without censoring the information. That being said, it's up to me to interpret what the data means. One of the most common ways to receive information, whether it be from your guides, deceased loved ones, angels, or even your higher self, is through symbolism. Using psychic symbols, which should not generally be confused with ancient symbols or hieroglyphics, is an easy way to communicate a message.

Symbols can come through to you via any of your psychic abilities. It's a language we can all understand, regardless of how we normally receive information in our daily life. It is much simpler to convey an idea, a thought, or even a concept by showing us a picture of something. It can be a visual picture or an audio clip. It can be a feeling or just a knowing. No matter which gift you perceive the symbols with, they offer you a fuller picture versus just a word or two.

A symbol can be one simple line drawing, like a paisley design, or it can be more complex, like a street complete with lights and sounds and movement like the Las Vegas Strip. There is no limit to what type of symbol you can receive. The only limitations are ones you put on yourself. Utilizing your imagination—that part of your mind that can develop images, thoughts, and feelings—can help you understand what each psychic representation can mean. Often, we try to block out our imaginations to allow only pure intuitive messages to come through, but by doing that we also block out a way to interpret and clarify the information we are given. This cuts down on our proficiency to translate our psychic symbols. Rather, learning to decipher by using our own tools, like our imagination, helps us provide a better reading or unravel what we receive for ourselves.

EXERCISE
· ·
Gathering Cues through Imagery

It's time to use your imagination to understand exactly how much information you can gain from just one symbol. You don't need any special tools for this, but if you'd like to write down the information you garner from the following symbols you can!

As always, take a deep breath and relax. Put down anything you may have in your hands and allow each finger to relax as well. Close your eyes and continue breathing in and out, allowing positive energy in and negativity out. Keep doing this for at least one minute or until you feel comfortable.

Now, imagine, in your mind's eye, a hotel lobby. It does not have to be one you've been to; it can be any hotel lobby. First notice the basic size of the space. Is it large, small, or medium sized? Does it open to hallways or other areas? Is it closed off? Now, visualize the overall color. What color stands out in the room? Is it everywhere? On the walls? The floors? The furniture and counters? Do you see any signs or logos? This does not have to be a sign stating the hotel's name, but any signs or words that you may see? Take a moment to catch up to yourself and answer all the questions above.

Now, what color is secondary? Is it a similar shade to the primary color you first imagined? Or totally different? Where do you see this color? How does the color make you feel? Happy or sad? How about the overall feeling in the room? Is it comfortable or friendly? Is it stark or unfriendly? Does it feel inviting and warm or does it make you want to run out the door? Do you hear any sounds? If so, what are they? Do you hear people talking or yelling or laughing? Do you hear music playing? Do you hear some-one tapping on a computer keyboard? Or children crying?

Next, pay attention to your sense of smell. Imagine what the lobby smells like. Is it a fresh scent? Does it smell musty? Does it have a bad odor? Do you smell something familiar? Can you smell something cooking? Do you smell a certain perfume or cologne? Notice whatever you can about the way it smells.

When you are all done and have gathered whatever information you can about this particular hotel lobby, take a moment to determine if this is somewhere you've been before or something you made up in your imagination. Either way is totally fine. Just recognize it for what it was. If you want, record all the information you gathered from this exercise in your notebook. Review it. Did you imagine a lot or a little? Were you able to visualize using all your senses, or was one more dominant than another? Was there anything that surprised you? Or made you feel uncomfortable about going into your imagination? If so, note what it was and examine why it may have made you feel that way.

We're not done! You are beyond beginning so you need to go deeper. Think about the colors you saw. Who or what do they remind you of? What about any of the fur-niture or the artwork or signs you may have seen? Do they make you think of someone or something? How about the sounds you heard or the scents you smelled? Were any feelings provoked in this imaginary hotel? Did it jog your memory of somebody? Or maybe a time in your life or a significant event? Think of all the cues this imagery gave you and pay special attention to which sense seemed to bring more relevance.

. . . .

Using your imagination allows you to be open to interpreting messages with greater clarity. The more you practice this exercise, the easier you may find it to understand any symbolic impressions you receive. Being able to visualize using all your psychic senses will illuminate the messages in a way that allows you to figure out exactly what the message is.

When Symbols Are Literal, Metaphorical, or Both

So often we search for meaning in every thought, idea, or vision and we think it is a psychic symbol or a sign to be translated. Sometimes the images we receive are symbolic. Other times, they are simply true representations of a message we are being given. And, still other times, they can be both. For example, if I am doing a reading for someone and they ask me a question like, "Who do you see me with in my next relationship?" I can ask for some direction from my guides on the other side to send me a message to help answer them. If I then see, psychically, an image of a garbage can, it's up to me, and my client, to decipher what this means. One translation may be that the person will literally be a garbage man. Going deeper into the symbolic realm could indicate she will be with someone who will not be good for her, or who might treat her like garbage, or the person she is currently with is someone who needs to be thrown out. And, it could indicate all the above. It's about the ability to interpret the information by giving what you get, without judging or censoring it.

If you receive messages you can't readily decode, you can ask for more information. Requesting clarity on what you perceive often helps to refine the symbolic data you've been given. Using the garbage can example, you or your client may be left wondering what the message was supposed to tell you. Should your client be on the lookout for garbage men to date? Or should she interpret the message that she needs to discard the person she's with? Asking for additional symbols can help with that. If you are shown a garbage truck, in addition to the garbage can, and possibly even a road, chances are your guides are trying to share the client's next relationship will be with a garbage man. Soliciting additional information should become second nature, as this is a simple way to provide you with deeper, beyond beginner, extrasensory guidance.

My sister Tammy called me out of the blue yesterday, just to chat. We started talking and she said she was having a rough day and needed me to tune in to her for an impromptu "in-the-moment" reading, which is something we often do for each other.

"Okay. Well, this is kind of funny. I'm seeing a sidewalk. Are you walking on a sidewalk, like near a parking lot or something?" I asked her.

"Hahaha, yes I am!" she replied. "I just left school."

My sister is a psychotherapist and an adjunct professor at a college. She had just finished teaching a class and was headed to her office.

"Hmmm. I think there's more to this sidewalk, though. I think there's a message here," I continued.

"Go for it!" she answered, always ready for a reading.

"I feel like where the sidewalk and parking lot meet is symbolic of what's happening in your life," I tell her.

"Well, what does that mean?" Tammy asked. "Is that like some kind of metaphor or something?" she laughed.

"Funny, but no. It's more about releasing what no longer serves you. Cleaning out the gunk that gets trapped along the edges of your life. There are issues or things happening that you don't want to deal with, so it gets pushed to the corners and avoided. It's time to look at these parts of your daily life and address them. Clear them out, systematically. You can't keep ignoring what needs to be dealt with because it's building up and causing you stress. Get rid of what you don't need anymore and let go of anything that's been dragging you down," I shared, almost rapid fire to her.

"Wow! I get it," she said. "As a matter of fact, I was just discussing this with one of my therapist friends yesterday! I was saying I have too much stuff that's holding me back, preventing me from moving forward."

"Great! I'm so glad it makes sense to you. It was pretty clear," I told her, and we went on to discuss what she could do away with immediately to alleviate some pressure.

When I initially saw the sidewalk and Tammy validated that she was actually walking in the parking lot, I could have stopped there. It would have been perfectly acceptable to keep it literal. After all, it was definitely a psychic hit. But, taking it a step further and reading it symbolically allowed me to provide her with a reading that gave her suggestions to move forward and make some significant changes. Interpreting the sidewalk as a symbol offered her options she could work with, rather than just providing

Tammy with the aha moment of evidence that I saw her on the actual sidewalk.

When we receive information it often comes through in bits and pieces. You may have experienced images showing up like photographs. Usually we don't have a dead person having a conversation with us as you would when you talk to your best friend. That type of communication is very rare. As a rule, we get messages in snippets that we have to put together. It is from these fragments that we're able to assemble messages.

Sometimes we don't just get information symbolically; instead you may receive a literal image and a translation is not necessary. Usually, there will be a backstory that this image may represent. When I did a reading for Marie, I kept seeing the Brooklyn Bridge. As a rule, bridges typically represent connecting to something or someone. They are very symbolic of connecting to the other side or to a deceased relative. But, with Marie, my helpers were trying to get me to reference Brooklyn, where Marie grew up. By showing me the Brooklyn Bridge, they helped me provide Marie with that aha moment where she knew we were truly connecting. So, in this instance the bridge was more than just symbolic, it was literal.

Amy came in one day for a reading and was hoping to not only connect with her potential, but also her deceased loved ones. As with any reading, I try to do what I can for my clients and hope the person they want to connect with comes through. Having said that, I don't always know how they will appear, and more important, what they need to share with me to prove to my client that it's really them. But, Amy knew. She had come prepared.

During the reading I kept seeing an image of a turtle. It didn't stop. A lot of other information was coming through as well, so I pushed the turtle away. Toward the end of the session Amy asked me if I was getting anything from her mother. Immediately I saw the little turtle again. I didn't know why, but at this point I knew I had to mention it.

"Why do I keep seeing a turtle?" I asked Amy. "I know you're asking about your mother, but I'm not really getting anything. I just keep seeing a turtle."

"Wow. That's perfect. That's exactly what I needed," Amy replied, looking misty eyed.

"Really? Are you serious?" I returned. I wasn't sure what was happening.

Amy reached into her pocket and pulled out a little pewter turtle.

"This represents my mom. She loved turtles and she gave me this before she passed. I told her if she was going to come through today, she needed to talk about the turtle to let me know it was really her."

Spirit works in mysterious ways. After thinking she wasn't with us during the reading, Amy's mother had indeed come through with evidence that proved she was present. This time the turtle was real, it was tangible, and I could hold it in my hand. As solidly physical as it was, it also symbolized Amy's mom. Just because you perceive something as symbolic, don't discount that it may be concrete, and vice versa. Always explore your messages in both ways to determine what they are communicating to you.

When I do readings I always present both options to my clients. Going deeper helps take the session to beyond a beginning-level session. I tell them what symbol I receive literally and ask them if it holds meaning for them. Then, I also share what it may mean symbolically, as I did with my sister and the sidewalk. Often, there is a duality in the messages and they are given to us so we may interpret them for our clients both ways to give them a broader reading. Sometimes it is just one or the other, but presenting them with both allows them to be part of the interpretive process. It also offers them the opportunity to ponder everything about the symbol, even if they don't understand the entire message until later. As always, be open.

Symbols Journal

Regardless of what level you are on, creating your own symbols journal is an important way to remember and recognize what psychic symbols may mean for you. When you receive something symbolically, it is up to you to translate it and everyone translates symbols a little differently. Because you are the one receiving the symbol, you need to be the one who can interpret it. By creating or updating your symbols journal, you provide yourself with a reference you can use.

At this point in your development, you may have already begun a symbols journal. Whether you've kept it in your mind or you've written it down, you've created it. Going beyond a beginner's level means translating symbolic information that's even more complicated. On top of recording a single object in your journal, it's time to record actions, situations, or events. If you receive a symbolic message of someone running, determine what that means for you. It could be as simple as you need to go running or your client is a runner. Or it may suggest needing to speed up or run away from a situation. Paying attention to what else is happening around the runner gives you a fuller picture and can indicate a symbolic situation. This is your symbols journal. It is what you determine, psychically, your symbols mean. This can come from a combination of what you already know about the object or situation added to what you intuit about it. You don't have to be right—you merely have to use your gifts. This is the information you want to record in your symbols journal.

EXERCISE
· ·
Making Your Symbols Journal

Get a blank journal or open a new file in your computer. Look around. Write down everything you see, leaving enough space to record the meaning after each word. If you are in the living room, for example, you might record couch, rug, television, piano, bookcase, book, picture, vase, and so on. Write down what's around you.

Then, go back to the first thing you wrote down. Using your intuition, tune in to the object and record what you think it may represent. For instance, couch may mean relaxation, rest, respite, living room, family, comfort, or putting something on hold. For your journal, it's what it represents to you. Continue translating all your objects.

Now, take it a step further. Imagine someone playing the piano, or painting the picture, or reading the book, or even a scenario of a party happening in the space. Create different events and situations in your imagination and write them down. Then, translate them using your psychic abilities to focus in.

When you are done with your immediate surroundings, think about other situations you can translate and write them down. Perhaps these are communications you've already received in the past, or perhaps they are new ones. Whatever you can think of, you can interpret. The sky's the limit. Continue until you are tired and then review what you've added to your symbols journal. Does it make sense? Do any of the interpretations surprise you? Was it comfortable doing this exercise or did you find it difficult? Remember, you can always go back and update your translations as your psychic abilities expand.

. . . .

This journal is for you. It can be shared or held tight to the chest; it's your choice. Symbols are one of the most common means of psychic communication and are therefore an important form to study. It is a fundamental part of developing your abilities and a key feature in taking your gifts beyond a beginning level.

Signs

The beginning of every psychic journey contains some telltale signs—literally. We start noticing signs all around us and ask for signs to help us with questions and guidance. Even those who claim they don't believe in psychic abilities believe in signs. Signs are similar to symbols but are tangible and physical like Amy's little turtle. As you progress beyond a beginner level on your intuitive journey, you will come to expect to receive signs daily. There are many different types of signs that will show up to help; you need only pay attention.

Symbols and signs are not mutually exclusive. You may find you receive both types as forms of psychic communication—symbols are generally the intangibles while signs are the tangibles.

Going beyond a beginning level, past simple messages, will open you up to translating complex signs and symbols. Being open to your psychic gifts in this way can increase your abilities and when you use complex messages it swells your senses exponentially.

When you are a beginner, just starting to work with your intuition, the presence of signs can be quite surprising, if you recognize them at all. As you move to a level beyond beginning, you won't be quite as shocked by them, but you may be astonished by how multi-layered the signs become. For example, you may ask for reassurance that your deceased mom, Norma, is with you from the other side as you're driving in your car. As you come to a stop, you notice the license plate in front of you has the name Norma on it. That alone is enough to convince you, but wait, there's more. You pull into a parking garage and there is a sign that says, "Be Sure to Look Above" and as you do you see the ceiling has been painted with angels. Finally, you walk into the store and the spotlight item on sale immediately after you enter is angel food cake. These are more complex signs, a continuing message that's answering your request.

Signs, as with any tool, should be used to help you in a variety of ways and for diverse reasons. There are different types of signs: here to help, guidance, and decision signs are just a few.

Here to Help Signs

These are signs from your loved ones, guides, angels, and the universe, to let you know they are here to help you. The signs they send to let you know they are around can be simple, like feathers or butterflies, or more particular, like seeing the same exact purse your mother had that you used to root around in when you were a child. Take these signs as shout outs to you from the other side. They are letting you know they are around to help you with something or that they see what's happening in your life.

Guidance Signs

We all need some guidance on occasion. We receive signs to help us decide which way to go or determine whether our intuition is on the right track. When looking for a new career, we may ask for a sign to show us what we should pursue. Maybe we'll be drawn to look at a billboard that has a new career path. Or, we may be online and get bombarded with ads for job headhunters, which can be interpreted as a sign to look to someone else for help in changing careers. These are signs that the universe is sending us to help guide us in the direction we need to go.

Decision Signs

Trying to make a decision can be one of hardest tasks. Getting a sign to assist us in making that decision can ease the burden. When a decision just needs a "yes or no" or "stop or go" answer, it can come to you in a simple way. For example, someone e-mailed me after reading my book *The Book of Psychic Symbols*. They were trying to decide on whether to move or not. In other words, should they stay or go? She told me she was thinking about this and asked for a sign. She was driving down the road and had to slam on her brakes because there was a stop sign lying in the middle of the road. That was a pretty clear sign about what to do— she was staying put.

The more advanced you become with your psychic abilities, the more signs you'll recognize. They will also become more multifaceted, bringing clarity with each additional tangible message. The universe always sends us signs to help us on our path or to acknowledge or guide us; you will notice them frequently as your gifts grow.

Receiving the Message

Whether a symbol or a sign, this form of psychic message is sent in your direction to assist you. As your psychic abilities grow, so too does your comprehension of both tangible and intangible messages. Your increasing awareness of symbolic communication will naturally enhance your intuitive senses. Recognizing more extensive signs will enhance your metaphysical knowledge. Allowing both avenues of communication furthers your abilities to beyond a beginner level. As your perception develops, the energy you tap into will strengthen as well.

. . . .

CHAPTER 3

Energy, Power, and Chakras

You are no stranger to energy if you've been working with your psychic abilities already. However, you may have been working without protection. Understanding how energy works is the gateway to better controlling how you use it and how it affects you. It is the connection we have to the universe and allows us to connect to our intuition as well as the other side. Energy is the medium on which symbolic and other messages come through. Learning to manage our energy helps us balance our chakras and influence our auras in a way that will stimulate your gifts past a beginner level. Protecting your energy and learning how to really work with it is a crucial step in developing your metaphysical powers.

Energy can be as simple or as complex as you let it be. Electrical energy works when you complete a circuit of positive and negative or grounded energy. A battery works by connecting the positive pole to whatever you are trying to power, like a flashlight, and then it connects from a different point on the light back to the negative pole. When the circuit is completed, it will power the light. When it is interrupted in the positive or the negative return, it will shut off or extinguish the light because the energy is cut. This energy is something you can control with a switch. You can witness it visually, only because of what it produces, when you see the light turn on or off. You can instantly see the energy working. Electrical energy is simple once you know the basic principles. Psychic energy is simple too; you need only know how to work with it and what it feels like to experience it.

Yesterday, my dishwasher would not turn on. It bothered my entire household. My husband, who is a high-end custom woodworker, is also a jack of all trades. So, of course I was counting on him to fix it. Well, it turned out it wasn't the dishwasher at all. He determined it was electrical and traced the problem through three different outlets, a circuit breaker, and my kitchen lights. Many hours later, he was able to fix it. However, the fact that a wire had come loose in our wall, which could have easily started a fire, made me stop and think. This tiny wire had interrupted our energy in a major way. It forced us to change our plans for the day; it disrupted our lives. It could even have been catastrophic. But, by grounding the loose wire, we were able to rebuild our own energy and salvage the day. Our intuitive senses work in much the same way. When you are not grounded, it can stop you dead in your tracks. When there is an attack on your psychic energy, even the smallest one, it is felt and can change your psychic abilities in a profound way.

Protecting Your Energy

When you are distressed in any way, it changes your energy, whether it's physical, mental, or psychic. Physical energy can easily become depleted. When we exercise for long periods of time, it can exhaust us. You can become tired when you work too hard mentally. Stress can drain your energy as quickly as running a marathon. It's the same psychically. When you get overloaded with other people's energy or take on too much, it can be psychically exhausting. Empaths, or people who feel other's energy to the point of taking it on themselves, can become especially fatigued, and often feel the effects through their own moods changing without apparent reason. Psychic attack happens when someone consciously or even subconsciously sends negativity your way with or without the intent of causing you damage. Often, the one attacking doesn't even realize they are doing it. Whether from someone living or someone who's passed, protecting yourself from psychic attacks and from energy that's not yours is essential to keeping your own energy unpolluted.

There are a number of ways you can tell if you are being psychically attacked. Though, be careful—more often than not, these symptoms may be due to other external or internal influences. Don't automatically attribute the following to psychic attack without exploring other solutions.

You might:

- begin to experience emotions that come out of nowhere
- start doubting yourself
- experience random headaches
- experience lethargy or a feeling of total exhaustion
- feel like you are constantly being watched or you always look over your shoulder because it feels like someone is there

- have nightmares

- have an overwhelming feeling of anxiety

- become extremely pessimistic

- feel claustrophobic

- feel uneasy or physically sick

- have angry outbursts

The list can go on and on, but essentially psychic attack will feel negative or as though you are being dragged down into something unpleasant. The best or safest method to unburden yourself of this sensation is to clear your energy and protect yourself from attack.

EXERCISE
. . . .
Protect Yourself

Regardless of where you are on your psychic path, a good dose of protection will assist you in going beyond. The more you practice, the more natural it will be and the less effort you will need to exert. Relax and breathe. As always, being somewhere quiet will help you concentrate. Take another deep breath. Imagine beautiful silver tubes coming out of the bottoms of your feet. These tubes connect deep down into the center of the earth. Now, imagine also a large sunflower-shaped showerhead reaching down from the sky above you. Breathe in again.

Visualize in front of you a big toggle switch marked "On 1/On 2/Off." When you are ready, reach out to the switch and move it to the "On 1" position. You might immediately feel a tingling on the bottom of your feet as the silver tubes start their process. These tubes are negativity vacuums. They are getting stronger as they continue. They are drawing the energy that no longer serves you or that you no longer need down into the earth to be recycled into positive energy.

With every breath feel the vacuum working, starting from the soles of your feet, moving up through your legs and into your hips. On the next deep breath, feel the vacuum move up into your abdomen, sucking out any negativity. Feel the draw of the silver tubes clearing out everything you don't need to hold on to anymore, anything you've taken on that's not yours. Feel the vacuum move up even further now, into your chest. Allow it to pull out the energy of anybody else you've taken on that you don't need. Release any negativity or psychic debris that has been trapped in your heart and let it flow into the earth to be recycled. On the next deep breath, move the energy up through your throat, into your jaw, and release anything that no longer belongs there. And, with one more deep breath, allow any feelings that aren't yours, anything you've been holding on to, anything you've been thinking of, to be pulled out from your face and head to the tips of your hair, to flow down through your vacuum.

Sit with the vacuum for another minute, allowing every nook and cranny to be cleared of any debris. When you feel like all the energy you don't need has been vacuumed out, take another deep breath.

Now that you've cleaned out all the energy that doesn't belong to you, it's time to protect yourself. As you inhale, reach your hand out and flip the switch to the "On 2" position. Imagine the flower-like showerhead above you turns on. It's showering you with warm, silver, protective rain, gently spilling down over you. As it surrounds you, it provides protection from any energies that don't belong to you. Feel the silver energy encompass you, giving you strength and shielding you from taking on other people's stuff. On your next deep breath, feel the silver rain coming out of the showerhead envelop you like armor, armor you can bring with you wherever you go.

When you feel fully protected and fortified with the protective silver rain, turn the switch back to "Off" knowing you are shielded from any conscious or unconscious psychic attacks. Any time you need to bolster your armor, all you need to do is visualize that showerhead spilling positive energy over you.

. . . .

What Energy Can Really Do for You

Much of psychic ability is intangible. When we receive psychic energy via the clair senses, we can't physically touch it. Rather, the information is perceived psychically. We receive impressions. These impressions are transmitted as energy. And although we can intuitively feel these impressions, we can't hold them in our hand. It's the energy we experience, not a tangible, physical item, person, or place.

Every living thing is connected energetically. This energy, the energy of the universe, is what allows us to tune in to our psychic abilities and discover the metaphysical side of life. With every step in your awakening process you increase your energy overall, which means you need to either expand your cosmic footprint or you have to channel that energy into something. When you don't do one or the other, you become stifled and lose momentum. Instead, take advantage of this growth cycle and release the boundaries that may have restricted you from increasing your gifts. By tapping into this energy, you can connect to your intuitive self.

Connecting to your metaphysical self does not mean cutting off the energy from everyone else. While you don't want to absorb the energy of others, you do want to be able to understand the energy you pick up psychically from those around you. Being able to discern the difference, and not holding on to the issues of others, is what will separate your psychic gifts from possible psychic attack. To comprehend the psychic message being communicated, you sometimes need to assume their energy—this is fine as long as you release it when you're done.

While not always easy to recognize, taking on the energy of others does happen occasionally when I do readings. It happened most recently during a session with Pia. Before my client comes into my office, I normally sit down and meditate on them for a couple of minutes. Then I write down whatever information I receive so I can share it with them. On this day it was different. I felt foggy and couldn't focus.

"I'm so sorry. I feel like I'm in a fishbowl or something. My brain feels foggy. I feel like I wasn't able to tune in to you like I usually do," I told Pia.

"Oh, well, that's okay, I guess," she replied, a bit unsure.

"Let's just go ahead and start. Hopefully this confusion will lift soon!" I continued, asking for my guides to give me some clarity.

I went over everything I had written down. We had many hits, but it seemed we were missing something.

"Did someone pass from complications from a motorcycle accident? I'm getting a motorcycle, but I'm feeling they didn't pass from that."

"Oh, I think I know, but are you getting anything else?" Pia asked.

"I'm sorry, again! I feel all fuzzy. My brain feels like it's in a cloud. All I got was a motorcycle and then a year or two passes. Does any of this make sense?"

I felt bad. I was trying. I knew Pia wanted to connect with someone she'd lost, someone who was very important to her, but I couldn't pull myself out of the weird stupor I was experiencing. I explained that I was happy for all the information that I was able to share with her, but that I might have to cut the session short.

"Actually, it makes perfect sense. My dad was in a motorcycle accident. He didn't die immediately, he was around for about a year and a half. But, he suffered a traumatic brain injury as a result of the accident and it was like he was always in a fog. That must be why you feel spacy!"

"Wow! Thanks for clarifying. I thought I was going crazy. I was ready to stop the reading."

Pia's dad had come through for her. He'd been trying to come through even before she got there, I just hadn't recognized it. He was sending me his energy, having me feel a bit of what his life was like before he passed. It felt disconcerting to me, because it wasn't my energy. Yet, it was difficult to surmise exactly what happened. By assuming his energy, I was able to bring solace and relief to Pia, letting her know he was around her and he loved her. Sometimes, we get lucky—we realize what energy really can share with us.

Chakras

We all have a subtle but powerful energetic system that connects our physical sense to our spiritual sense. These are our chakras or our spiritual batteries. We have seven of them beginning at the base of our spine, running up in a rainbow-colored line to the top of our head. Popular author and instructor on chakras, yoga, and more, Anodea Judith, shares, "Chakras are organizing centers for the reception, assimilation, and transmission of life energies ... [and they] form a mythical *Rainbow Bridge,* a connecting channel linking Heaven and Earth, mind and body, spirit and matter, past and future."[3] To really become enlightened, it can take a lifetime to balance these energy centers. We are going to begin, balancing your chakras to increase your proficiency of using them to your advantage. The first step is to learn and identify which energetic blocks or obstacles hold you back from achieving balance. If you are already familiar, it can be useful to reexamine your connection to realize blocks that may have been previously overlooked.

Before every reading I do, I have a ritual. Whether I do an office or phone session, it's usually the same. I sit down and do a quick meditation to stimulate all my chakras and get them flowing. This helps me balance and open them to receive information

---

3. Judith, Anodea. *Wheels of Life: A User's Guide to the Chakra System.* 2nd ed. Woodbury, MN: Llewellyn Publications, 2006.

I can understand and share with my clients. It also helps ground my energy, so I can be present enough to perceive the messages and astute enough to translate them to meaningful data my client can recognize. This meditation can also help to alert you to anything that is getting in the way to allow clear communication.

Opening your chakras is an integral part of receiving psychic communications from the other side. From your root or first chakra at the base of your spine, to your seventh energy center at the top of your head, your chakras run in a straight line in the color of the rainbow. The challenge is not in trying to find them; it is in stimulating them enough, and in the right way, so they can be balanced and open and of use to you in your psychic work.

EXERCISE
. . . .
Lighting Up Your Chakras

No matter what your experience level, this exercise is a constant necessity in your psychic life because your chakras will always need your attention in order to best serve you. Go somewhere without a lot of distractions. Sit or lie down comfortably and close your eyes. Breathe deeply. Focus on the bottoms of your feet. Imagine there are roots reaching down to the ground, growing out of your soles. Feel these roots grow as they make their way down to the center of the earth, attaching themselves to a boulder down deep. As you continue to breathe, feel the energy of the earth reach up, through the roots, into your feet. You may feel a tingling sensation, or you might experience warmth.

Allow that energy to travel through your legs, up into your calves and shins. Feel the warmth as it spreads through your knees and up into your thighs. When it reaches the base of your spine, imagine a bright red, beautiful sphere of energy spinning like a wheel. Pay attention to how this root chakra spins and direct it to balance so it spins evenly, creating a steadier foundation.

Let that energy move up a few inches below your belly button and imagine this second chakra emitting a bright orange color throughout your abdomen as it spins. As this sacral chakra balances, it will increase your sensory abilities, allowing you to feel and interpret messages. As it spins, it discards any negative energy that may have become attached. You may also feel a clearer, more balanced sexuality, opening you up to increased sensuality. Once that orange chakra is spinning freely, move the energy up.

Your third chakra, located in your solar plexus, is next. Imagine a brilliant yellow disk, bright as the sun, rotating while driving out any imbalances or negativity. As it turns, feel the warmth spread, extending outside your physical body. This is the seat of your intuition, your gut instinct. Enable this chakra to open and balance as it rotates, allowing you to feel the energy around you.

It's time to charge your fourth chakra, located in the center of your chest. Move your awareness up, into your sternum. With your psychic vision, see your heart chakra emit a luminous, gleaming green color. This is your healing center, your love and caring chakra, and it needs to be balanced so you can honor yourself as well as others. With every heartbeat, feel your fourth chakra strongly pulse and allow that energy to continue upward into your neck and throat area.

On your next inhale, picture a radiant blue light beaming from your throat chakra. This area rules communication. As this chakra rotates, any need to share information with those on this side and on the other side becomes easier, and the ability to receive and decipher messages is heightened. You may experience a tightness in your throat area as any negativity is released and your energy center spins freely.

Allow that brilliant energy to continue rising into your third eye, the space between your eyebrows. Feel your sixth chakra spin, emitting a stunning indigo light. Focus your attention here; as it spins it releases any negativity and opens your clairvoyant sense. Allow this energy to continue rotating and balancing. While this beautiful indigo center gets brighter, you may feel a temperature change in your forehead. Sit with this for another moment and then move the energy up.

Feel the top of your head, your crown chakra, as the energy opens it. Feel that area revolving, swirling, and sending out a tremendous brilliant violet color. As your energy increases, spin away any blockages, allowing your psychic abilities to open. You may feel a tingling sensation in your crown chakra as your intuition gets recharged. Visualize this purple color expanding and streaming out all around you.

Sit with your eyes closed, reveling in this feeling while your seven major chakras continue to whirl, releasing any negative energy that has accumulated. When you feel your chakras are balanced, take a few deep breaths and open your eyes. Feel a sense of peace as it washes over you, grounding you, balancing you. Sit and relax, enjoying this feeling for a few minutes.

. . . .

Now that you've opened your chakras and begun balancing them, you may experience a rise in your kundalini, your potential life force energy. Kundalini is a Sanskrit term from ancient India that identifies a natural and powerful energy we have at birth. "Kundalini energy rests like a coiled serpent at the base of your spine ... As your kundalini energy rises, it passes through each of your chakras and awakens human potentials lying dormant until activated."[4] Author and metaphysical practitioner David Pond explains that through breathing practices and meditation, we can set in motion this chi or life force energy.

When Chakras Are Out of Balance

Countless people associate opening chakras with having them balanced. This is only partially true. Opening, clearing, and balancing them goes a long way toward having a healthy mind, body, and spirit system. But chakras can get blocked when they are too open as well. If a chakra remains wide open, it can also hinder elevating your psychic gifts. If a chakra is excessively open, it can

---

4. Pond, David. *Chakras Beyond Beginners: Awakening to the Power Within.* Woodbury, MN: Llewellyn Publications, 2016.

create a fixation with the properties or elements of that chakra, or if one is consistently closed it may trigger avoidance in that area.

For example, the first chakra relates to your foundation, your structure, and even your childhood. So, if it is wide open you may find you are constantly thinking about yourself or your material possessions and even believing you are above others. You may also feel you are indestructible and will always be taken care of, even to your own detriment. If it is continually closed, you may be very introverted, non-trusting, and hold a belief that you're never going to be safe or secure. You may also feel you will never be quite good enough.

If your second chakra is wide open, you may find yourself channeling everything through your sensuality or even your sexuality. This may give you an unhealthy heightened sex drive, and produce the idea that sex is power, or that sex is control. You might find the only way to connect to others and feel in charge is through your sexuality. You may be driven to fulfill your sexual needs by channeling all energy through that chakra center, which will cause an extreme imbalance in the way you view all situations. If this chakra is blocked and closed, you might be afraid of entering into any intimate conditions and refrain, even vehemently, from any type of sexual contact. You may be fearful of sexual advances, to the point you withdraw from the situation or relationship.

Your third chakra is your power center. If it's disproportionately open, you may find yourself constantly arguing or confronting others; in fact, you may thrive on it. You may feel the need to be correct, or believe you're always right, regardless of the facts. Challenging everyone can become your way of being. If your solar plexus chakra is blocked because it is closed, you may run away from any type of confrontation. You may panic at the thought of defending anything you believe in and might even consider yourself wrong more often than not, so you find you give in habitually.

Having your heart center, or fourth chakra, extremely wide open might cause you to be overly sympathetic to the plight of others, even if that means damaging your own life. It can also create the idea that everything is about love, and that being in love is more important than being compatible in a relationship. The idea of love, above all else, is what drives your thoughts and communications with others. If this energy center is closed, you might experience a constant sense of loss. Feeling as though you have to protect yourself and your heart can cause you to keep others at a distance and feel somewhat detached from society. Being closed can cause you to distrust other people and might even create a lack of empathy or sympathy.

Communications can become one-sided when your fifth chakra is off. When this throat chakra is open wide, so is your voice—you may talk too much and not listen to what anyone else says. Even if you remain quiet during someone else's narrative, you still talk in your mind and are unable to focus or hear the other person speaking. Alternatively, if this energy wheel is closed tight, you may find the cat has your tongue or you are tight-lipped and even afraid to speak up. With a blocked fifth chakra, you will find it difficult to get your words out and might even find yourself saying nonsensical things.

The third eye, the seat of your clairvoyance, when stuck wide open can cause you to have frequent daydreams or even hallucinations. Your imagination may run wild. You might even see ghosts that aren't there. When this sixth chakra is fixed open, you may suffer from too much physical light—both artificially from lamps or natural sunlight. Your eyes may burn and want to close, though the images and brightness will continue to penetrate. Having a sealed up third eye can create a world that is darker, where you dream less and are unable to envision or imagine anything. It will keep you from utilizing your clairvoyance and hinder your attempts to connect psychically.

Finally, the crown chakra, seated at the top of your head, helps you feel linked to your psychic gifts. When your seventh chakra remains wide open, you may feel spacy and out of sorts. You will experience people and events in a surreal way and might find yourself channeling energy that doesn't belong to you—both positive and negative. You will often feel distracted or disoriented. When this wheel of light is shut tight, you are closed off to divine or psychic guidance. You might feel alone or even lonely and disconnected from the energy of the universe that connects all living things. It can also cause anxiety or worry. You may even feel heavy and lethargic.

Working with your energy centers and focusing on each one individually is a surefire way to increase your psychic abilities. Your gifts will open at a glacial pace without tapping into and stimulating these spiritual batteries. Your chakras help you experience joy and happiness, which is crucial to motivating your gifts to expand. Raising the overall frequency of each area will improve your chakra's function. Scanning your energy, on a physical level, will help you determine which centers need work.

EXERCISE
· ·

Body Scan

Go somewhere quiet where you won't be disturbed. Take out your journal and your pen. When you are done scanning, you will write down everything you experienced.

Part One: Beginning with your root chakra, focus your attention on the space at the bottom of your spine. Note how that area feels. Does it feel distressed in any way? Or does it feel content? Is it warm? Cool? Burning hot? Freezing cold? How does that area behave? Does it move freely? Feel stuck? Once you're done with your root chakra, continue scanning through the remaining six, asking the same questions.

Part Two: Now it's time to think about your chakras and how they relate to your daily life. Using the examples of chakras that are stuck open or closed, reflect on each individual energy center and how it works. Think about its function and what each wheel regulates. Ponder each individual chakra and determine whether you feel they are balanced or out of sync, noticing how each chakra felt in part one. If you ascertain any of your energy wheels need work, decide how you can improve each one. For example, if it feels like your fifth chakra is too open, you may need to work on listening rather than talking.

Part Three: Address each chakra, one by one, and devise a plan of action that you can put into place over the coming weeks. Take your time with each energy center to be sure you give it enough attention to fully increase its performance. You can change your actions, your thoughts, and even your diet to adjust and fix the balance in each chakra. Think of the color of the chakra and the colors of the foods you eat. If you feel your second chakra is off and you don't eat enough orange foods, you may want to add carrots to your daily food intake. Alternatively, if you eat red meat, red candy, and strawberries at every meal and your first chakra is overflowing, you may want to cut back. And, finally, write down all your discoveries. Include your findings from each part, by chakra. Be sure to record your action plan for each chakra as well.

. . . .

Your chakras deserve attention. Coordinating your chakra training with your other intuitive practices will help you satisfy your psychic development goals. You'll discover working with the energy within and from your chakras will amp up your auric energy and help propel you to a new level with your abilities. Your next move may be life-altering and multiply how quickly you progress.

Auras

It's doubtful you've gotten this far in your development and not heard the word *aura*. Everyone has a metaphysical aura and this natural energy field can be manipulated and used to heal, tune in to your gifts, or reach out to someone locally or distantly. Our body is our physical presence and our aura is our metaphysical presence—the energy that normally projects from our corporeal body about one to six inches and, with minimal training, can usually be seen with the naked eye. Auras can pick up and send out energetic vibes and messages across the globe and to the other side. Learning the basics about the auric field is easy; essentially every living thing has one and it is part of what makes us who we are and helps us to bond with others. Using our aura as a critical tool in our psychic development can mean the difference between playing with your gifts on occasion and being in the groove and really rocking it.

The aura is a powerful and very useful component in our psychic growth process. By expanding your native field, you increase your energetic footprint. The aura contains layers of wisdom and knowledge that you can transmit or receive psychically, using your extrasensory abilities. We feel our surroundings by using our aura much like insect antennae would sense objects or predators around them. It is one of the psychic first responders and lets you know what's happening when you walk into a room—it can pick up on energy and instantly present you with a sense of joy, fear, anger, happiness, or more. It can work as a receptor to enhance your psychic perceptions.

When working with your aura, you are able to receive impressions about a person, their mood, or their current state. You may pick up names of people around them or situations they are going through. Think of your aura as a way to filter information from the other person's aura, information they are often unaware they put out. You can easily connect and read others using your auric reach. This is an important process to develop your psychic abilities beyond a beginner level.

An easy way to feel your personal auric field is to hold your hand about an inch away from your other arm in a relaxed manner.

You should be able to feel a difference in the air between your hand and your arm. This difference is the energy you naturally project. This is your aura and, as I said, it can be pushed further out to send your ethereal field and expand your presence. Auras can also let you know if someone is in your energy in some way. If they are thinking about you or reaching out to you, this is often where you'll feel it. It can also be where you feel a psychic attack; if someone is doing you wrong it might present in your auric field by making you uncomfortable in your own skin or giving you bad vibes, even if you don't know what's going on.

Feeling the aura is one way to experience it—seeing it is another. Generally, the aura is translucent, but within that translucence it is very colorful. These colors can be read to interpret what is happening with you in the moment, and the colors can and will constantly change and morph into other colors. There are many books that will help you decipher specific colors, including my *Book of Psychic Symbols*, but, quite simply, if you see the colors, allow yourself to interpret how they make you feel. For example, red generally represents fiery energy, even angry or powerful, forceful energy, whereas a beautiful light turquoise blue may make you feel serene or happy or relaxed. By interpreting the colors you see based on how they make you feel, you'll be able to decipher the auric impressions you pick up from yourself or from the auric field of other people.

Assuming you already have some experience working with auras, the next exercise should help you further develop that skill. Rather than just trying to read someone else's aura, you will also try to project your auric energy out to someone else. For this exercise there are two different options, and you can play with both.

EXERCISE
. . . .

Working with Auras

Option One: Ask a friend to join you at a neutral, quiet place. You want it to be neutral because you don't want to pick up on the energy from the location attached to either person, you just need to focus on the auras you project instead. Get comfortable, seated about four feet across from each other. Decide that you will be the receiver first and your friend will be the giver, but allow that you both receive impressions.

Consciously connect to your aura by closing your eyes and focus on the area surrounding your physical body. Concentrate on the space about one inch away from your skin, your aura. Have your partner think of an emotion. They may want to think of a circumstance when they felt strongly about something, either positive or negative. Then, have them push that emotionally charged aura toward you. Have them take a deep breath and push it out even further, expanding their aura. Stay like this for a few moments, both of you feeling the emotion.

When you believe you've felt enough and your partner is ready, open your eyes. Intuit what emotion they sent out. Did you receive what they sent? Were you able to psychically pick up the emotion? Could you read your friend's aura?

Don't be discouraged if you didn't. If your friend sent frustration and you said anger, those are pretty close. If you felt excitement and your partner sent happy, that's okay, too!

Take it a step further and have them send an emotion through color. For example, if emoting anger they might want to project red. After you're done, swap jobs and you convey an emotion and color to your partner. Are they able to receive the information psychically? Which way worked better for you? Receiving or sending?

Going beyond a beginning level, work on psychic messages. Have your partner think of something in their life or something they want answers to and transmit that information out toward you through their aura. Imagine the data is floating within their auric field, available for you to pick up. Using all their energy, have them push it out as far as they can. As they do, notice anything you receive. You may intuit words or images or sounds or even colors. Let them know whatever you get. Does it have anything to do with what they thought about?

Keep practicing, reversing your roles. You can also try to sit closer to each other to see if that increases your ability to psychically read each other's auras.

Option Two: This one is a little more delicate, and you need to be sure to only try this with someone you are close to, as it can feel a bit invasive. Think of someone in your life—significant other, best friend, and so on. Randomly try to tune in to their aura to pick up what they are feeling or what they are doing in that moment, no matter where they are. Expand your aura with the intent of connecting to their aura. Once you feel like you've joined with them, intuit whatever you can from their energetic field. Imagine you can see, hear, feel, and even taste everything there.

When you're done, try to immediately get in touch with them to tell them what you did. Ask them if they felt your attempt to connect. It may have made them feel they were being watched, or they might have felt heavier or as though they weren't themselves. This is normal. Share with them whatever information you psychically gathered and see if they can validate what you received.

. . . .

While beginners may learn to see auras, going beyond that opens you to reading the aura by accessing the information we all transmit, either intentionally or unintentionally. Once you begin deciphering the messages beyond the colors, you will notice a more heightened psychic ability. This naturally produces a more advanced metaphysical intelligence. It also contributes to unearthing your power.

Focusing on Energy to Awaken Your Power

We all have greatness deep down inside us. It is there, possibly undeveloped, but definitely abundant, just waiting to be discovered. Bringing that power to the surface is merely the beginning of your psychic awakening. Mastery does not come quickly. It comes with practice, effort, and the desire to go where you have not gone before. To go deeper, really digging into your energy to find your power, will connect you to your dynamic self. And then there will be no stopping how far you can take your psychic abilities.

So, just what is it that makes you powerful? Everyone is different. Our sense of personal power depends upon what drives us, what makes us whole. Our power is what gives us strength to persevere and go beyond a simple beginning. Without our power, we would never be capable of transcending a basic level. Raising our vibration aids us with that transcendence and increases our metaphysical intelligence.

There are different ways to awaken your power. But, before it can happen you have to believe in the possibility that you are, indeed, powerful. Rhonda Byrne shares in her book, *The Power,* that to be in your power you must come from a place of positivity and love. By shifting how you function in life you can increase your power. "Change your frequency at any time by changing how you feel, and everything around you will change because you're on a new frequency."[5]

Often, we've given away our power. To reclaim it you must set the intention to get it back or to release that part of you to rebuild it more positively. Your third chakra is the seat of your power; it is where you establish your feeling of self-esteem, self-image, and confidence. Also known as your solar plexus chakra, this area can cause your energy to be depleted when you are feeling inadequate. To awaken your power, you need to balance this chakra.

Trying to control everything, from your family and friends to your coworkers, can cause this chakra to go out of balance. Much like working from your ego, this unbalanced, lopsided chakra also affects your psychic gifts; the need to control how everything works and what comes through creates a disruption in the flow of information. By misdirecting your desire for self-control, you are

---

5. Byrne, Rhonda. *The Power.* New York: Atria Books, 2010.

diminishing your capacity to command your power. When you seek to control others you are, in fact, giving them your power.

My daughter was having a discussion, via text, with her teammates. They were trying to decide on a picture they would get for senior night, the night the whole team, and the entire audience, gives the seniors recognition at their last home game. Theoretically, the picture would have the graduating year and the names of the seniors along with a representation of the sport. Not a big deal, or so one would think. The people in charge of picking the picture began arguing over the merits of one design over the other. It got a bit nasty. When my daughter showed me the choices, I noticed the differences were insignificant. I asked her what she wanted.

"I'll go with whatever," she answered.

"You aren't arguing with them?" I questioned.

"No, I don't really care. Either is totally fine. I don't need to control it," she responded, with nonchalance.

"Great! Because they're trying to control the situation. Such a little thing, but they're exerting so much effort just so they can control it."

The more they tried to control the choices the other girls and boys were making, the more they gave away their power. In the end, it didn't matter which design they chose, they'd moved on to the next decision—hopefully without messing up their third chakra. By choosing to go with the flow, my daughter retained her power and kept her solar plexus chakra spinning.

Feeling out of control weakens your personal power. When you are faced with situations or people that are critical, or even hostile toward you, you can be deeply affected. Occasionally you can healthily walk away and brush it off, but if it feels personal, your usual response will be one of three options or even a combination: (1) you can allow their actions to make you dive deep into feelings of insecurity and poor self-esteem, (2) you can become angry toward them physically or even spew nastiness about them behind their backs, or (3) you can direct angry thoughts or negativity toward them.

The first, letting them pierce your self-confidence, creates a powerless feeling. It can even invoke memories of previously being hurt. By the very nature of withdrawing into yourself, you allow their actions to devalue you and your power to be further diminished. Through their unpleasant manipulation of your emotions, whether imagined or real, you've given away your power. You've released some of your energy, which is taking away from your ability to utilize that energy to enhance your psychic gifts.

The second, although it may feel like you've taken charge, is just an illusion. The reality is you haven't addressed the feeling of being out of control, you just reacted to it. And this reaction can cause you even more damage. You've deceived yourself into believing that by matching their actions and being combative, you step into your power. However, you are using up so much of your energy to be angry that there's no room left to be powerful. You are participating in a war—and there are no real winners in war, only casualties.

The third option involves sending negative thoughts into the universe to attack the person who caused you grief. Sending negativity out to someone may feel like the most passive and the least invasive to your own energy. However, think of energy like a boomerang. When you send it out, eventually it will come back. This option, though seemingly less aggressive, can do long-term damage to your power and can weaken your energy. This is the law of the universe—when you intentionally hurt someone with your thoughts you also injure yourself. You unwittingly injure yourself and your own energy, as it will rebound with an even greater force back to you.

Malia came in about five years ago. She was a beautiful spirit who hoped to increase her psychic abilities through training and practice and was willing to put in the time necessary to give it her all. She already had a strong foundation, so we were both excited to get her beyond her beginning level. We agreed to a mentoring program and began working together.

Every week between sessions, I'd give her homework to help her increase her psychic abilities. I'd done this plenty of times with others, so I knew it was a good way to have her practice. But, Malia's results were not quite what we'd hoped. She seemed to be moving backward and we had to figure out why.

When we had our sessions, Malia connected to her gifts and she excelled at every exercise. This told me we were on the right path and that she had the capability to expand her gifts. This was totally different when she tried to connect on her own. I thought maybe she was not able to stay focused when she was alone, or that she wasn't trying hard enough because there was no one there to hold her accountable. But, this didn't really make sense either. So, we had to figure out what was keeping her from advancing.

"Do you feel like you're connecting to your gifts when you're with me?" I asked her during our office session.

"Yes! I have no problem with my psychic abilities when I'm here. I just can't seem to get it together when I'm home," she replied.

"Are you able to focus? Like, really focus on what you're doing? Are you being distracted?" I pushed.

"I think so? I mean, usually no one's even around to distract me. My kids are in school or out of the house and my husband and I are separated. He doesn't live with us anymore," she responded, and I detected the slightest bit of irritation.

Now, this made me think. The kids being in school while she was working on increasing her skills was good. But, I felt a nagging thought that there may be a connection with her and her spouse that was causing her a hard time.

"Tell me about your breakup. I don't mean to be blunt, but I feel like this may have something to do with what's holding you back. You are naturally gifted, that's for sure; I would have thought you'd progress much more quickly than you are," I continued.

I was beginning to realize her block was not something she was even aware of, so I was hopeful to hear what she had to say.

"Well, it's okay. I mean, I'm pretty much running the show and have total control over what's happening. Even though my husband was cheating on me, we've gotten through it enough that I don't hate him," Malia told me.

Aha. Now we were getting somewhere.

"Tell me, when you come in, are you thinking about your husband? What he did or even your living arrangements?"

"Um, no, I don't think so. I wasn't thinking about him before you brought it up. Why?"

"And, when you're home, trying to work on yourself, are you thinking of him?"

"Yes, I guess. I have to construct visitations, a financial plan, and even dates with him, even though I'm still not sure what I want to do. I alternate between being angry at him for breaking up our family and wanting to get back together with him to mend our family. I have some wicked thoughts, that's for sure, but I'm in control of the situation. Whatever I want to do he'll do, because I told him he needs to keep it together or we're definitely done," she answered.

"That's it. That's what's happening. You just said you're having some wicked thoughts. That means, and correct me if I'm wrong, that you're sending some negative energy his way, probably when you're home alone. When you do this, you get back negativity even stronger. You are also trying to control everything that's going on, even him, and that's diminishing your strength. It's taking away your own personal power, which means you're not bringing enough to the table when you're working to bring your psychic gifts to a new level. Rather than increasing your abilities, you are manifesting undesirable energy. Imagine your power like your shield and the negativity is like little arrows that are being shot at it—it's distracting and it's weakening your power," I explained to Malia. "I think this may be the problem!"

After we figured out what was going on, I devised an exercise she could do every time she worked on her own. She was able to increase her gifts after doing this on a regular basis. It's a simple exercise, but a strong one! That, coupled with the termination of intentionally sending out any bad thoughts toward her husband or anyone else, changed her life.

EXERCISE
· ·
Releasing Negative Energy
to Advance Your Power

Sit somewhere comfortably. Close your eyes. Breathe deeply until you're relaxed. When you are ready, continue breathing while you imagine holding a wooden box in your left hand. This box is about ten inches square and is light enough to not weigh your hand down. In your right hand there are several black strings reaching away from you. Breathe in again and feel the heaviness of the strings and the lightness of the box.

Now, think of the last time you sent a negative thought toward someone. It doesn't matter who it was, and it really doesn't matter why. Imagine that thought as one of the black strings and begin reeling that string in. As you inhale, coil it up and then, on your exhale, release the negative energy and place the string into the wooden box. Move on to the next black string and think of a recent time you felt you needed to be in control, even though it wasn't necessary. Take back your power by reeling in that string. Place it in the box and blow in positivity as you do. Continue assigning each string to a time you gave away your power in some way, releasing the negativity as you pull them in, and breathing positive energy into the box.

When you are finished, feel how your right hand, previously holding what you put into the universe, has become incredibly light. The box filled with the power you've taken back has become weightier, filled now with recycled positive energy. Place your powerful box against your solar plexus.

Feel your third chakra spin, balancing out now that you've recalled your energy. As you do, notice the box becoming lighter and lighter. You are welcoming the positive energy into your power center. You may feel a vibration growing, getting stronger—this is good! Enjoy the sensation.

Once the box feels almost lighter than air, it's time for you to take another deep breath and open your eyes. You are stronger now, filled with the power you've gotten back, armed with plenty of energy to awaken that power to be used to develop your psychic gifts.

· ·

The act of calling back the daggers you've sent toward others into the universe and releasing the need to control a person or situation does not negate the original intention. It does, however, change the energy and create a more positive platform for you to work with. When you remove the pessimistic feelings, you create the space to allow your power to reside. This, in turn, helps give you more control than you had before. The illusion you had of being in charge when you were sending out negativity is shattered, and you can begin to awaken and step into your own personal power. You are now allowing for a greater foundation to jump-start your psychic gifts to the next level.

Negative Energy Is Not Always Bad

Negative energy is not always toxic. Positive energy is useful for expansion and moving forward. But negativity can direct you to stay clear from something or someone who may be detrimental to your growth. The negativity that comes from disappointment or even disillusionment can be a gift that keeps you from making a big mistake. Paying attention to all the energy present can lead you to your perfect purpose or your truth.

Negativity can remind you there is something holding you back. It might show up because something feels off or wrong. It can also be your cue to check yourself and any bad vibes at the door. If you find yourself complaining a lot, take a minute to figure out what is bothering you or what is at the core. Remember to always discern whether you are taking on someone else's energy, especially if you are empathic. You might be experiencing negativity from outside sources. It may also reveal someone who is wishing ill will upon you, which will alert you to their true intentions. If you are feeling negative, it may simply be a reminder to change your direction.

We all experience disappointment when something doesn't go our way or as planned. When we don't get what we want or what we expect, it can be hard to get past it. If we don't get the job we think we need or the boyfriend we have been pining over, there may be a reason for it. Possibly, the job would have prevented us from getting the even better job that was coming in a week. Or going out with the boyfriend would have kept you from meeting and falling in love with your future partner. Thanking the universe and your guides for *not* getting what we want advances our opportunities for receiving what we need. Recognizing this comforts us in our disappointment and opens the door for more beneficial gifts and possibilities. And, even more important, it's another link in the psychic chain—helping to connect you to the universal energy and to your guides.

Experiencing something other than positivity can happen because you step out of your comfort zone. This can be difficult and even unpleasant. But it also allows us to grow. As distressing as it may be, it can bring about positive change and help to expand our awareness. It can cause you to proceed in a new way that may be awkward, but can be a perfect opportunity to produce an abundance of gifts that may not have otherwise been there for you.

Another way negativity clues us in to what is going on with us is when we find ourselves in victim mode. "I'm not good enough." "I don't deserve it." "I will never have it." "I am not worthy of someone's time or love." "I am terrible at tuning in using my intuition and I will never get it." "I am not psychic." "I don't have an intuitive bone in my body." "As spiritual as I try to be, I just can't do it." These are all victim statements and they will most definitely hold you back from trying to accomplish whatever it is you are putting yourself down for.

So, now that we know why we should appreciate negativity, and we've practiced one exercise to change it, what else can we do? We know we need both positive and negative energy to balance ourselves, so we don't always want to get rid of negativity. We can't eradicate it, but we can use it to our advantage by understanding why it is there. And, we can change it. Here are a few ways to essentially turn that frown upside down and get ready for intuitive gifts and challenges to come your way!

EXERCISE
. . . .
Manifesting Positive from Negative

To change from negativity to positivity, you must acknowledge where you need to evolve in your intuitive life. What do you need to change or make better? Think of a situation where you feel you don't deserve to be successful (with your psychic gifts) because you're not good enough. Focus on that situation. Feel it. Why do you feel you aren't worthy? Is there a specific reason you feel you are not good enough? Where does the negativity come from?

Challenge it: Let's challenge that limiting belief right now. If you were successful, what would it bring you? Would that make you happy? Would it be positive? Can you envision yourself being psychically successful?

Change it: Change your perspective on the situation. Can you attain a different outcome if you approach it from a different direction? Do you need to use a different psychic gift? What if you change your environment, what you're doing, who you're doing it with, and so on?

Adapt: Maybe you aren't supposed to be successful at this particular juncture or with this particular situation. Possibly it's because you are focusing on a specific psychic component when you need to adjust your approach. If you change how you approach the situation (with more love or needing to be successful for a different reason), will you attain a positive outcome?

Let it go: If you still don't have a positive outcome from a negative beginning, maybe there's a lesson to be learned. Once you discover what that is, you will be able to move forward and manifest something that is, indeed, better for you!

Manifest it: Instead of coming from the negative position of victim, change it up and come from a positive place of winner! Manifest a positive outcome by asking for it, trusting it can happen, letting it go without trying to control the "how" aspect, and thanking your guides and angels for helping to make it happen. Give yourself weeks or even months and check back to see if what you hoped for has manifested.

· ·

One method from this exercise may not work. But, one of the others might. It is smart to try all the different approaches and determine which works for you with each particular situation. Often, the way we expect things to happen is not how they happen at all. This is okay. Expect that. Then, appreciate the negativity that balances out our positivity and helps to keep us grounded.

One Doesn't Work without the Other

Negative energy and positive energy are both useful. You need the balance. Working to change and adapt negativity to positivity will transform your psychic gifts, bringing you to the next level of development. You can't talk about energy without discussing chakras, and vice versa. Chakras are a major part of your personal energetic system; they are what feeds our auras (the ethereal energetic layer we can project toward the world) and what allows us to raise our frequency so we can connect to the other side and our intuition. Coming into our power is about raising our own personal energy and discovering how to handle negative and positive situations to our advantage helps to awaken our power. Utilizing all the energetic means to elevate our psychic abilities is a crucial component to move beyond a beginner level. And, you'll discover just how much you are energetically connected when you raise your vibration.

. . . .

CHAPTER 4

Break "Beyond" and More Easily Access Your Psychic Gifts

Getting to the place where psychic ability flows easily is the ultimate goal. It starts with the desire to be psychic, and then continues with a fundamental need to develop your gifts. Though it is not a step-by-step process, there is a basic order to things. This chapter, you'll discover, offers you a transitional period and the tools and direction you need to increase your psychic intensity. Going within to access your gifts is critical. This allows you to travel using your spirit and to raise your vibration based on your thoughts. To make it an easier transition from a beginner level to beyond, you need to take stock of what you've been thinking about. It's a good time to reflect on what you believe and what interests you and your spirit.

Raise the Vibration of Your Thoughts

We create our own reality. Our thoughts design our lives; whether they help you or hinder you is the question you must ponder. Another way to understand this is to realize that what we pay attention to becomes the focus of what our life is. Just think about what that means. When we pay, we invest in something; there is an expense. When you direct your attention to something, it makes that more prevalent and pulls your consciousness to it. It is important to pay for something or manifest something you want, rather than get distracted by that which will not serve your greater purpose.

Having said that, it doesn't mean that just because you decide one day you'd like to be psychic, you automatically will. It does, however, create a greater possibility that you will increase your skills. What we surround ourselves with is what shapes us. If we choose to be around others who don't believe in the psychic reality, we may stifle our own development; it can take a toll on our own thoughts and make us doubt the validity of what we are trying to accomplish. When, instead, we join the ranks of all the people around the world who trust in the absolute of intuitive existence, we elevate our own gifts and can immerse ourselves in this psychic world. This, subsequently and collectively, raises our vibration and helps us increase our metaphysical skills.

Raising our vibration is a true gateway to psychic development. Empowering ourselves to believe we can go to a level beyond helps propel you to that next degree of proficiency. Getting to that point, past where you've been before, takes nurturing. You need to cultivate your energy to grow your psychic gifts. Sometimes it helps to visualize what it would look like to raise your vibration—seeing it will often help you to translate it into the thoughts you need to produce the results you want.

EXERCISE
· ·
Raising Your Vibration Layer by Layer

As usual, get comfortable and take a few deep breaths. Close your eyes and breathe some more. Stay in this space, with your eyes comfortably closed and continue inhaling and exhaling, relaxing with every breath.

Imagine a thick, delicious, multi-flavored seven-layer cake in front of you. The bottom layer is vanilla cake. Gluing this to the layer above is vanilla frosting. Starts off pretty basic, right? But, nevertheless, still delicious and moist. Take a bite! The next layer is a confetti layer. There are sprinkles melted into the vanilla cake and on top of that is a mouthwatering strawberry frosting. We are building a delectable confection! Are you still eating? Above that is a sheet of marble cake, with fudgy chocolate mousse icing on top. Eat it! Is your mouth watering for more? Mine is. Luckily, there's so much more.

Next, there is a chocolate layer, with cherries and black forest cream followed by a sheet of coconut cream cheese-cake with coconut cream cheese icing. This is getting intense! Yum, that tastes amazing. The sixth layer is a delicious blend of almond cake and oranges with a whipped-cream topping. To cap it all off, there's a red velvet layer with a purple grape and plum frosting. This is a crazy cake! I just swallowed my seventh bite. How about you?

Now, go back to the bottom layers. Vanilla, simple but appealing. Did you stop there? Or were you able to rise to the next layers? They were a little more developed and interesting as you expanded with each flavor. Think of the cake layers as your psychic vibrational layers. Were you able to build it up? Or did you get stuck somewhere?

How did it feel? Did you want to stay at one spot in the cake because it was familiar? Did it spook you a bit to imagine a flavor that didn't quite make sense to you or that wasn't as comfortable as the other flavors? Was your attention lost at a specific layer? Perhaps halfway through?

Go back and imagine the cake again. Now that you know how raising your vibration can relate to moving up the cake layers, was it easier to imagine and visualize and even enjoy each layer? Or do you still stop somewhere? Maybe substitute the layers with something you've always wanted to try but were afraid to because you thought you wouldn't like the change. Take that bite, make the connection. Was it difficult to imagine going where you've not gone before?

. . . .

Obviously, this cake metaphor is about raising your vibration, but it's also about changing your mind-set. When you accept that you can challenge yourself to a point you've not gone before, you are able to expand your psychic talents. Increasing your frequency gets you that much closer to moving beyond a beginner level.

Meditation and Mindfulness

Meditation is a fantastic way to help raise your vibration, thereby helping you connect on a deeper level to your psychic abilities. Meditation is a state of deep relaxation and can be as easy as taking a simple breath. By directing your intention to your breathing, you are guiding your conscious mind to lead the way for your subconscious to begin processing and healing without your conscious input. All that's needed to meditate, to reach a state of detachment from the external self, is to allow it to happen. Relaxation of the body can assist the mind to reach a safe zone, where nothing can hurt or control it. This can, at times, be difficult to achieve, though taking that first deep breath is the best way to start.

Meditation has many health benefits, such as lowering blood pressure, reducing stress, decreasing anxiety, and helping you sleep better. Meditation can alter the way you react to run-of-the-mill happenings, which in turn can bring a sense of peace. Serenity can be achieved in the moment, but also for the long term. The more often you meditate, the easier it becomes and the more it transforms your way of being. Knowing how to reach a basic meditative state is the first step toward reaching a spiritual awareness that can bring you to a level beyond beginning.

Many of us already have a meditation practice, or at minimum, have some experience with meditation. All meditation is good meditation, but all meditation is not practiced with the same goal. Meditation is mostly used for relaxation, which is a wonderful first step toward using meditation to enhance your psychic awareness. Once you've discovered how incredible meditation can make you feel, and what your current meditative habits can do for you, you are ready to expand your routine to include meditation to enhance your extrasensory gifts.

Meditating helps you empty your mind from conscious thought. We typically have so much static playing in our minds that it can block the inflow of psychic information. When we quiet the chatter, we are more receptive to messages. Learning how to mindfully meditate allows us to silence the constant distractions and be present in the moment. It will bring you a sense of peace and calm, enabling you to link to the universal energy with your extrasensory gifts without consciously interfering.

Jon Kabat-Zinn (author, biologist, and creator of Stress Reduction Clinic and the Center for Mindfulness in Medicine, Health Care, and Society) describes mindfulness as "paying attention in a particular way: on purpose, in the present moment, and non-judgmentally."[6] Mindful meditation does not come easily. Rather it may take quite a bit of exploration before you feel you are truly meditating. Practicing will help get you there.

EXERCISE
. . . .
Mindfully Meditate

Go somewhere you won't be disturbed. You'll need a good amount of time to practice, so allow for that. Sit or lie down comfortably. Close your eyes. Begin by focusing on your breath. Feel the oxygen as it enters your nose, travels down into your throat, and into your lungs. Then, focus on the air as it leaves your mouth. Be in the moment. Focus only on your breath. As other thoughts enter your mind, acknowl-

---

6. Kabat-Zinn, Jon. *Wherever You Go, There You Are: Mindfulness Meditation in Everyday Life.* New York: Hyperion, 1994.

edge them and let them go, transferring your mindfulness back to your breath. Every thought you have is merely a distraction. Continue breathing until you feel more focused than distracted. When you are ready, move on.

Now, bring your mindfulness down to your pinky toes. Feel them. Breathe energy into them. Focus on where they are on your body. Feel your blood flowing through them. Feel the temperature of them. Feel where your toenails connect to your toes. Feel where your toes connect to your feet. Feel where they touch your other toes. Once you've connected to your pinky toes, take another deep breath and move your awareness up to your calf muscles.

Feel the energy flowing through your calves, blood and energy pulsing through with every breath. Feel the power your calves bring to your legs. Feel the strength in your calf muscles, ready to be utilized on command. Be present and bring your entire focus to these muscles. Stay there for a moment, until you're ready to move on.

Next, move up to your hips. Feel the way your joints connect. Focus on the area between your hips. Be mindful of how your pelvic area feels in this moment. Notice the warmth in your lower abdomen. Pay attention to how your insides feel; notice if they feel heavy, light, and so on. When you have explored and focused entirely on your hip and lower trunk area, you are ready to move up.

Focus your energy on your entire torso. First pay special attention to the exterior of your body. Then, when you inhale, focus on the processes inside your body. Sit with this large area and allow yourself to focus on every bit, a little at a time. Feel your muscles contract as you breathe and your chest fills with oxygen. Stay here until you are prepared to move up into your neck and shoulders.

Move your attention to your spine, where it enters your neck and shoulder area. Pay attention to how it feels, whether it feels loose or tight, stiff or flexible. Concentrate on the muscles there and be mindful of what they feel like. Contemplate on the joints where the shoulders meet your collarbone and notice what they feel like. Then, travel into your head.

Focus on your head, the entire head. Your face, your muscles in your face, your mouth, nose, and eyes. Then pay attention to the top of your head, your scalp, and even your hair. Feel your ears and how they reach inside, down to your throat and the side of your head. Feel your jaw muscles and your cheeks.

When you've explored your face and head, take a deep breath. Continue breathing and focus on your breath as it moves through your nose, and into your chest and lungs. Pay attention to how it feels as it leaves your body through your mouth. Keep your focus on your breathing as the air travels in and out.

Bring your mindfulness to how it feels to have your body sitting or lying down and take a few more deep breaths. When you are ready, open your eyes and bring yourself back. Remain in the present.

....

Mindful meditation helps provide us with a glimpse into our own life, our own energy. It offers us an opportunity to get ourselves unstuck and get out of our own way, imparting to us a greater awareness of reality in the present moment. Meditation also helps you connect to your spirit. It allows you to enhance your connection to the energy that connects us all. Through this link you may even begin to travel psychically and be present metaphysically in another place or time.

Psychic Abilities, Meditation, Hypnosis, and How They Connect

You may think psychic abilities and hypnosis are two very distinct specialties, but in reality, there are many areas where the two overlap. Hypnosis is similar to meditation but requires a very definitive stated goal before executing this type of guided meditation. And, you already know that meditation can allow your conscious mind to take a back seat, permitting you to remain open to receiving psychic messages. So, utilizing these available tools and learning how they connect will help you become more proficient with your intuitive gifts.

When I discovered my propensity for intuitive abilities, I began to recognize I wanted more. I wanted to understand how people had memories of other times and how these details from these other lifetimes were popping up in my readings. I began studying hypnotism and became certified as a hypnotist. I realized I could offer more than just readings when I discovered past-life regression hypnosis and how it played a part in discovering who we were in this lifetime. Another way to gather metaphysical data is through astral or psychic travel. This type of extrasensory journeying can be achieved when combining hypnosis and meditation with our psychic gifts. This method of being in another location spiritually, while your body remains physically somewhere else, can be accomplished and used to gather psychic information. Learning these more advanced practices will help you increase your psychic abilities to beyond a beginner level.

Meditation and Astral (Psychic) Travel

People dream when they sleep. Most often these are dreams that seem fantastical or unreal. But, many people have dreams that feel very real. This may be due, in part, to visitations. Loved ones and guides often come through during sleep because you are, essentially, out of your conscious state and they can get through without you doubting or blocking them. Also known as psychic travel, astral travel is another way physical reality, normally not visited, shines through in your dreams. This can leave you feeling like something was more real than just a dream. Your spirit, traveling out of your body, is able to visit other people or places and experience things while your physical body remains asleep. Most often, this happens without any conscious effort or decision. There is a way to achieve this level of astral travel or have an out-of-body experience while awake. This enables you to gather data in a metaphysical way, different from when you consciously use your senses and try to bring the information to you.

Astral travel can advance your psychic abilities in a way nothing else can. It can allow you to bilocate to a place distant from yourself in order to know what is there or what is happening there. This is also known as remote viewing. Having the ability to gather data from the other location can help you psychically perceive where lost objects or even people may be. It can assist you in viewing something you wouldn't otherwise be able to see. It can also assist you in psychically connecting to someone else.

Through meditation you can achieve psychic travel. When done correctly, you can project your astral body out of your physical body and travel to a pre-determined location or even a random spot. This can be achieved with practice and the belief that it is possible! Occasionally, it occurs when you least expect it, as it did with my client Delia.

Delia came in a few years ago wanting me to facilitate a past-life regression for her to discover who she was before she began her journey in this lifetime. This is a common request from my clients for a variety of reasons. They come out of curiosity, or they are searching for a reason or some background why they may have a phobia or fear in this current life. Frequently, clients are looking to understand why they are struggling with an unhealthy relationship with someone. They know why they are there and their past-life regression usually reflects it. Delia's session took a strange turn, though.

I began relaxing her, getting her ready for her past-life regression session.

"When I count down from three to one, you will step into a place distant in time and space, a place you may or may not recognize, that has everything to do with who you are today. Raise your finger to let me know when you're ready to begin," I told her.

She raised her finger and we began the process of acknowledging who and where she is. I ask her to look at her feet and her hands and even her clothing and to tell me what they look like. She answers, and her response makes me wonder if she's regressing at all.

"It's me. It's the same outfit I have on now. My wedding ring is on my finger and I can see my toe ring," she answers.

I am feeling possibly she wasn't relaxed enough to travel back in time. Maybe I can salvage the session for her, so I keep going, hoping we can peel back her experiences in layers. I ask her if she feels like she is sitting down (like in my chair) or if she is standing or walking.

"I feel like I'm looking down, almost like I'm flying," Delia told me.

"All right. Is it light or dark out?" I ask, my curiosity climbing.

"It's dusky, but I can see," she continued in a raspy, breathy voice.

"Tell me what you see," I encourage her, intrigued by the slight change in her demeanor.

"I'm a little winded. I feel a bit detached," Delia says.

"All right, can you continue?"

"Yes."

"Great, tell me what you see," I say again.

"It's strange. I'm looking at the roof of my car?" she utters, questioning.

"What else do you see?" I asked, captivated by her response.

"I see other cars, from above, like I'm flying over them. It's the parking lot here, outside."

This has me fascinated. Is she just remembering coming into my office? Is she having difficulty letting go of her reality? Or, is it something more? Instinctively, I ask her a question that, depending upon her answer, I know I can validate immediately.

"What else is there to look at? Do you see anything besides the vehicles?" I inquire.

I observe her questioning herself before she responds, so I encourage her by telling her, "It's all right. Just tell me what you see."

"Okay. I am seeing all the cars, still. There is a minivan pulling in and parking."

"Keep going," I tell her as I inch closer to my office windows. "What color is the van?"

"It looks like a silver or a light blue."

I look out the window and see the tail lights of a silver minivan that just pulled into a parking spot. As I watch, a mom and a young girl hop out.

"Is there anything else?" I ask.

"Yes, there are a couple of people now. It looks like someone with brownish hair and someone smaller with blonde curly hair."

That's exactly what is happening outside my window. I am fascinated at this point because I realize I have not led her into a past-life regression; rather I've brought her, through meditation, out of her physical body and into her astral body and she is currently traveling outside my office building. I decide to try one more thing before bringing her back.

"Delia," I begin. When I do past-life regression, I don't use their name as this can create confusion in their past lives. I elected to use it intentionally to see if it threw her off or not, but it didn't appear to. "Do you see any buildings?"

"Yes. I see your office building and the salon next door," she responds with more confidence, now.

"Can you travel over to my window and tell me what you see?"

Unbeknownst to her, I was standing in front of it, now, waving.

"Okay, give me a second. It feels like I'm moving through a dense fog."

"No problem, take your time," I encourage.

"I see your window. And I see a person, I think. Wait, I think it's you. You're holding your hand up or something."

I continued the session and had her go to the edges of the parking lot, but no further. I wasn't sure how secure she was at this point, and I didn't want to cause her any anxiety. My office is on a busy road and I didn't want her to be fearful heading out above any traffic she might encounter. After I brought her back to her body and out of her meditative state, we discussed what had happened. Unlike a dream or even a psychic vision, she was able to remember, in full detail, everything she had witnessed. Delia, like I, was shocked that she had experienced an out-of-body episode. She, of course, was curious as to why she hadn't regressed, but she wasn't quite sure what was going on. We went on to discuss what happened.

I explained to her that she had an astral travel experience and that I had never witnessed a client having one while trying to regress. But, I also shared that it was a really cool thing and now that she had done it, she should be able to do it again, even on her own, through meditation. I intuitively knew this to be true. A few weeks later Delia contacted me and confirmed that after many meditative attempts, she was indeed able to recreate her out-of-body experience and even validated what she had seen by going outside to confirm her visions of what was happening near her house.

I witnessed Delia's initial experience, one that was unexpected and unprecedented for both of us. I, too, have experienced a form of psychic projection or travel. For me, like Delia, I was not immediately aware of what was happening. I was participating in a week-long class to study remote viewing when I had my own out-of-body, astral travel experience. It was, in a nutshell, surreal.

I was at Omega, and the assignment was given to tune in, using remote viewing, to an undisclosed target. This meant we, as a class, were given the task to view somewhere or someone, but we didn't know where or who. We were told to do this overnight and come back the next day with the data we collected. The entire evening, and into the morning, I felt extremely uncomfortable. I felt like I constantly had to look over my shoulder because there was someone watching me or following me. I didn't like it and I didn't know why.

We shared our experiences in class the next morning. I shared that I felt strange. It felt like I was seeing things outside of myself, as though I were looking at my own actions with other eyes, even to the extreme that I watched myself sit at the dinner table with other students the evening before. It turned out the assignment was to remotely view ourselves! That, of course, meant that what I was actually doing, without realizing it, was psychically traveling and watching myself the whole time. I was the one that was making me uncomfortable, though I hadn't been aware of it. I was metaphysically traveling outside of my body, watching my physical self. That was my first experience with true psychic or astral travel.

Delia did it, I did it, and I am confident you will be able to do it too! You have the added benefit of already possessing a keen sense of intuition and are on your way to develop it further. Practicing doesn't always make perfect, but it will take some effort to learn how to astral travel through meditation. In the last exercise, you were tasked to do a mindful meditation. Before you move on to astral travel, make sure you are comfortable with the previous meditation. If not, do it again. There is nothing saying you can't repeat it numerous times to prepare for your out-of-body experience.

With Delia, there was no time to prepare for her astral travel. She began taking a random journey until I guided her to a specific location. For practical purposes, you would do better allowing a trip without a predetermined destination for your first attempt. At the end of the following exercise, you will have an opportunity to direct where you want your astral body to take you. But first, you can master, or at least attempt to master, getting out of your body.

For now, do not worry about gathering specific psychic data. Instead, just practice the spiritual journeying. You don't want to have to think too much about it during your first attempt. If you find you can travel easily, at the end of the exercise you will find direction to gather information about where you are, and as you continue practicing, you can allow for bringing more information back from each journey.

EXERCISE
. . . .
Astral Travel Meditation Part I

As always, go somewhere you won't be disturbed and be sure you are wearing comfortable clothing. Try to lie down instead of sitting as this will help provide a better probability of a successful journey. (I will refer to where you're lying as a bed, but you can be on the floor, on a couch, or even lying down in your car.) Begin by breathing deeply and continue focusing on your breath. When you reach a deep state of relaxation, you can move on.

Move your focus to where your heels are touching down against the bed. Notice how it feels to connect there, and then move up into your calves. Again, pay attention to where you are touching the bed and feel how you are almost being drawn down into the bed. Continue moving up your body, into your thighs, rear, back, shoulders, arms, and head, taking plenty of time to feel the physical connection where each body part touches the bed. Feel yourself grounded down, relaxed and content.

Imagine there are two sets of magnets. The first are attached to you everywhere your psychical body meets the bed—one positively charged on each area of your body and a corresponding negatively charged one in the same places along the bed. These magnets are creating a perfectly balanced connection, keeping your physical body attached to the bed.

Now, imagine a beautiful fluffy cloud. Within this cloud there are negatively charged magnets. More positively charged magnets are attached to your astral body, just above your physical body—above your toes, your knees, your hips, your abdomen, your chest, your hands, your jaw, and your forehead.

Feel the positive magnets attaching your physical body to the bed, repelling the positive magnets connected to your astral body—the two cannot connect and they naturally begin to separate. The cloud begins to float upward and starts to gently pull your astral body up with it. You may notice your forehead area being drawn up to the cloud first, followed by your jaw and your hands and your chest and your abdomen and your hips and your knees and your toes. Bit by bit, feel your astral body drawn out of your physical body up to the beautiful, light cloud. When your entire spiritual body floats up, it begins to mesh with the cloud, allowing your astral self to float without effort. It might feel as though your temperature has cooled down, almost icy. This is okay and is nothing to be concerned with. The ambient temperature of the cloud will keep you safe.

Imagine now that your cloud self turns over, gently, in a non-jarring way. Your astral body is now looking down at your physical self, lovingly, appreciatingly. Allow the cloud to begin carrying you. As you look down you can see what you are gliding over. Notice any colors you see as you slowly move. Pay attention to any shapes below you.

As you continue to move, observe where you may be. Are you still near your physical self? Are you in the same location you were when you started? If so, continue moving. If not, discern what you are looking at. Try to make out some particulars, like how far off the ground are you? Are you inside or outside? Are you nearby or have you traveled a great distance? Do you hear any sounds? Are there any people? Can you discern any details about what you are looking at? Is there anything above you? Allow your astral body, your spirit, to look for anything remarkable that you will remember when you get back to your physical self.

When you've satisfied your travel yearnings, allow yourself to float back, slowly. When you see or feel you are above your physical body, release the magnets holding you to your astral cloud carrier and allow your physical magnets to gently cradle your spirit back inside your physical body. You may experience a bit of a jolt. This is okay. Don't worry if it happens. Alternatively, it may feel as though your body has become wrapped in a nice, warm blanket. Take stock of how well you did with your, possibly, first astral travel experience.

Now, process your experience. Did you enjoy it? Did it feel comfortable? Were you able to travel? Did you feel you were out of your body? If you traveled away from your physical self, go and validate what you saw—the colors, shapes, sounds, people, and other details you discovered during your astral travel experience. If you traveled a great distance, too far to physically go right now, look the area up on the internet to help you validate it. If you can't get validation this time, it's okay, or if you didn't accomplish what you'd hoped, give yourself a day or two and try it again.

EXERCISE
. . . .
Astral Travel Meditation Part II:
Take Off to a Destination

It's time to travel once more, but this time decide on a destination before you go. For your first attempt, pick a destination you can easily validate by physically attending. You want to have access to the location immediately after you're done with your meditation. Choose a spot that may have some activity, but not too much. It's hard to verify the data you perceive in real time if there are constant changes.

When you are ready, repeat Astral Travel Meditation Part I. When you get to the part where you begin to move away from your physical body, set your intention to travel to your pre-determined location. Notice whether you can observe anything along the way. Pay special attention to the little details, even things as small as a cup on a table or even the color of flowers. It's these details that will provide validity to your traveling.

Allow yourself to freely travel to your destination; don't try to control how you get there. Once you've reached your location, examine what is there. What do you see? What do you hear? Do you feel anything? Are there any other people there? Does it feel warm? Cold? Comfortable? Uncomfortable?

When you are ready, come back to your body and gently release your cloud. Were you able to travel to your pre-determined destination? Was it very quick? Did it take a long time? Did it feel easy? Was it difficult? What, if anything, differed for you knowing you had a destination instead of just free floating?

If you couldn't accomplish this type of astral travel, no worries. Practice will help you. Go with whichever way felt better or easier for you. Having a specific destination right now is not essential.

. . . .

Astral travel can create a feeling of detachment. It may also bring about a feeling of being displaced or dizzy. Be sure when you are done practicing to pay special attention to how you feel. You may have to stomp your feet or go outside and hug a tree to try to ground yourself back into your physical body.

Getting beyond Your Ego

Perhaps you have been practicing readings and are feeling stuck. When you are at a point in your development where you receive more positive feedback than negative from the person you're reading for, it can make you feel pretty good. There's nothing wrong with this; in fact, it's wonderful. Getting validation that your readings are hitting home can fill you with a sense of pride, which again, is great. What you need to beware of is how easy it can be to lead with your ego instead of your intuition. The need to feed your ego by being right should never be your primary focus. Instead, your goal should be to provide the cleanest, truest reading possible, even at the risk of being wrong. When you work from your ego, you will never be communicating the truth and you won't be able to progress.

How do you know when you work from your ego rather than your intuition? You can tell the difference in a variety of ways. Your ego is going to look for external validation, to make sure you're right with everything. Your intuition, however, just knows. Though you desire validation from others when you read for them, the need for validation should never overpower the intuitive data coming through. Intuition is love based, whereas the ego is often cloaked in fear. Though the information you receive psychically may make you happy, it is neutral in form. The ego, on the other hand, is harsh and tends to make you feel less than or unworthy unless you do something strictly to pump up your ego. Your psychic self will not generally falter, unlike your ego, which has a greater capacity to change to fit your ego's idea of what something should be, even if it is contradictory to what you previously thought or felt intuitively.

Essentially, your ego is lying to you. It makes you distrust your true intuitive self. It pushes away your psychic gifts, making you doubt your abilities. It needs to be the best—if it's not allowed, it will feel threatened and cause you to lash out and create confusion, crashing down your psychic intuition. Your ego works hard trying to convince you that you need to be a certain way, and perfection is just a part of that. Eckhart Tolle, a worldwide spiritual teacher and author, says in his book, "I have also met many others who may be technically good at what they do but whose ego constantly sabotages their work. Only part of their attention is on the work they perform; the other part is on themselves. Their ego demands personal recognition and wastes energy in resentment if it doesn't get enough—and it's never enough."[7]

The problem with ego driving your intuition or anything else is that it prevents you from tapping into your psychic gifts. It holds you back, concerned with the possibility that you may be wrong or that you may not be the best. It shields your psychic birthright, falsely protecting it with the worry that if you let your ability shine, the ego will be attacked. Learning to identify when it's your ego or your intuitive self will allow your psychic gifts to flourish. It will help keep your psychic work genuine and brings your authentic psychic self to the surface so you can access and develop it.

---

7. Tolle, Eckhart. *A New Earth: Awakening to Your Life's Purpose*. New York: Plume, 2005.

So, how can you know whether your insight is coming from ego or intuition? When you think of various attributes, you might automatically recognize which are your ego and which are your intuition. When you're unsure, try tuning in to your intuition and let your psychic self feel which it is. To get an idea, here are some emotions, traits, and feelings to consider.

Generally, these come from your ego:

- anger
- anxiousness
- distress
- doubt
- a sense of emptiness
- fear
- harshness
- hollowness
- thoughts that jump around
- negativity
- doubt
- rationalizing
- having to be right
- feeling weighed down

These come from your intuition:

- feeling complete
- consistency

- creativity

- sense of freedom

- feeling fulfilled

- joy and happiness

- a sense of just "knowing"

- love

- feeling neutral

- positivity

- relaxation

Think of a person giving you a pat on the back. Is he encouraging you or pushing you down? These are your intuition and ego, respectively. If it feels right and comfortable and natural, chances are it's your psychic self, but if it hurts or makes you feel bad, it's probably your ego. Believing you can access your psychic abilities on a regular basis is the foundation on which to build and develop your spiritual awareness. What you think matters.

As you may have noticed, this chapter has been about getting you to a place where you can more easily access your psychic gifts. You may also have realized that a major step you need to take to get you there is to go within. Our thoughts create our reality. Now, I'm not saying that if you think you're stuck in a tornado you will actually be swept up with your home and belongings, but I am saying that you will keep feeling battered around. Thinking positive rather than negative thoughts will go a long way toward making you happy, which in turn will provide you with a sturdier platform to jump into your psychic gifts.

Meditation is a surefire way to direct your thinking and even to promote a stress-free way of life. You can access your spiritual self and tune in to your psychic abilities in an almost effortless process through meditation. Traveling from the comfort of your own home is made possible through astral travel, which opens your psychic abilities in a way you may have never imagined. And, maybe most important, is the discovery of how your ego tries to sabotage your gifts by creating a level of doubt. Your ego can also try to discourage you from utilizing every resource available to you, but you will learn that accessing your psychic gifts with the aid of tools will help you bring your gifts to a level beyond a beginner.

CHAPTER 5

· ·

Using Helpful Tools to Go Deeper

It's time to go deeper. When you start developing your psychic abilities, everything is new. Possibly you can intuit what someone else is thinking or that someone is going to call you soon. Maybe you've been psychically feeling things more often since you've begun. Perhaps you've connected to someone else. However, this was just the beginning. To move beyond the beginner's level, you need to go deeper into your gifts. Fortunately, there are helpful tools we can tune in to to get us there.

We could all use some help. Guides are the very definition of helpers. They are there to assist us when we know we need help, and even when we don't. The greatest thing about them is they don't want anything in return except our belief in them. We can think of our guides like tools—they make our psychic development easier when we use them. Tools are not necessary to access our psychic gifts, but we would be foolish not to take advantage of the benefits of using them.

Advanced Work with Your Guides

When you are first introduced to your guides, possibly through meditation, you may be excited, believing you know who you are permanently working with and that they, and only they, will always be there. It almost feels like a direct link to spiritual wisdom. This is great! But, it is not always the case. If you met one of your guides unintentionally, as in they just showed up one day or to help you in some way, that is also fantastic. But, again, it does not mean they will be your specific go-to guide or that they will always hang around to help you. The likelihood that this particular guide is going to be your be-all and end-all guide is actually very slim. However, you *will* always have guides to assist you when needed; they just may not always be the same ones. It's important to be open to all your guides.

Remember in chapter 1 when you were introduced to who you connect with? Let's take a more concentrated look at your guides: who they are and how they work with you. We each have an abundant number of guides, but we have some that show up to take you deeper, beyond your beginning. You've got guides that are with you throughout your entire lifetime, some even from lifetime to lifetime. And, you have some that come around to help you in specific situations or periods of your life. We want to connect with the guides that are there to help raise your vibration to a level where you can easily communicate with them and understand their messages.

At a beginning level we learn that guides tell us what we should do, either in general or in a specific situation. This is somewhat true, but not totally. When you move to a deeper level, you become aware that guides do not tell you what to do, but they help you see the bigger picture and possibly the most probable outcomes of any decisions you may make.

When I do readings for my clients, I ask the universe for information that can help my clients make decisions in their lives. I usually receive a balance of messages back from my guides and my client's guides that essentially point to my client's various options and choices they are free to make. I will psychically tune in to which may be better directions for them, but I won't tell them what they have to do. Just as your spirit guides won't tell you what to do, they will instead present you with options. It's up to you to take the risks or make the attempt to better your situation by paying attention to the, usually subtle, direction they urge you toward. Once you understand this, you can move to the next level with your guides.

Most people who connect with their guides do so on a very basic level. They may have met them through an exercise or intuited their name. They may have even asked for and received a metaphysical gift from their guide. This, the practice of meeting your guides, you can actually do on a daily basis because you will undoubtedly meet different guides and it's a great way to open your energy to the universe. Commune with your guides. Tune in to them and ask them any questions you may need answers to, not just about your psychic abilities, but about life in general. Your guides are there to make it easier for you to tap into your gifts to help direct you. They don't want to make it harder, so they will meet you at least halfway, you only need to put in the effort. To bring your meetings to beyond a beginning level, it's time to have a conversation. You need to begin to understand why they are there, what they can tell you about the universe, the way the universe works, and how you fit into it.

By connecting to your guides in a more advanced way, you will take your psychic gifts to a more advanced degree as well. It's fine to merely meet them, but to understand them is more profound. Think of it like a bicycle—your guide can tell you how to ride a bike, but it doesn't mean you'll know how to put the bicycle together or how it works. It's more about learning how to access the connections your guides help you with, so you can then use that knowledge to bring you to different dimensions in your journey.

I worked with Thea to help her increase her gifts. During one of her initial sessions, we discussed her guides. She felt that her guide, Sharia, was very instrumental to her psychic development. She went on to say that since she met Sharia in an exercise a few years prior, she had used her guide to answer questions for herself and others. I explained that while this may be true that Sharia is helping her, it was time for her to take ownership of her gifts and try to psychically connect without asking Sharia to do the work for her. But first, it was time for Thea to connect with Sharia so she could learn how psychic energy worked for her, specifically. Remember, we are all made up of energy, and with practice we can tune in to the universal energy that connects everyone. But, we will all do this in an individual, personal way. Thea agreed to try.

After she became relaxed in my recliner, I asked Thea to call out to her guide, Sharia. I wanted her to connect to Sharia specifically, as this was a guide she was comfortable with.

"Ask Sharia to come to you. Ask her to show up so you'll recognize that it's her," I instructed. "When she's there, let me know."

"She's here," Thea responded after a moment, and with a bit of awe.

"Great. What does she look like? What does she smell like? What does she sound like? What does she feel like?"

I wanted Thea to really connect to her guide. Paying attention to the details let her tune in with a stronger bond.

"She is very colorful, and she is kind of fluttery. She has a sugar cookie kind of smell. That's funny!" she began. "She sounds very melodic, like a beautiful flute, and she feels warm and soft."

"Wonderful. Ask her if she will help you learn on a deeper level today," I said.

"She just smiled. I feel like she will, as long as I'm ready to," Thea told me.

"Are you ready?" I asked.

"Yes."

"Okay. I will help you set the intention of what you'd like to accomplish today. What I say out loud, you can repeat in your mind to Sharia. She will hear both of us and it will make both our requests stronger," I told her.

She nodded in response. I knew from previous occasions that this might also allow me to experience some of what Thea would learn from Sharia.

"Hello Sharia. You've helped me discover my psychic gifts. I need you to explain or show me how the universal energy connects so I can do it myself without always depending on you to do it for me," I began and waited and watched Thea's face as I could tell she was repeating my words.

"I'd like to learn what I can in order to connect deeper, on a more advanced level, so please help me to understand," I continued. "Show me all there is."

Almost immediately, I began to see colors and sparks of light and energy in my mind. It was as though I was traveling through a twisting funnel that was bright and filled with a cacophony of colors. I glanced at Thea to make sure she was okay, and then let the journey continue.

"Bring me to where the answers are," I suggested.

I was happy to be on this journey with Thea and Sharia. The funnel of colors was opening. It appeared to be an entrance to a beautiful, vast, uncluttered area. As far as I could see there was an overall hue of blue and silver, with sparkly, almost prism-like, translucent panes melding with the entire space. I was looking at this, but, more importantly, I was in awe of what else I saw there. Free floating, almost funnel-like themselves, were beings of light. They appeared to be of the same shape, but varied in size, with a head and shoulder-like form that tapered down to an armless torso into a soft point, about where a human's thighs would be. There was nothing scary or intimidating about them, though they were very different from what I anticipated. Instead, the feeling I had was one of warmth and caring, generosity and love. Each being was floating next to a kind of small, round, modern-looking, whitish, lighted table, which was sharply tapered to a thin, brace-like support. It was freely suspended, as was the being.

Again, I looked at my client to be sure she was okay. I saw the telltale signs of her eyes moving under her lids, and her mouth, slightly smiling, was ajar in wonder.

I went back to the energy and saw on the closest table there was an open book, made of light. I could see a stream of energy going from the book to the being and I intuitively knew that this was information, and that this information could also be tapped into by humans to psychically gather data.

The scene started fading and as it did, I looked at Thea, and felt it was fading for her as well.

"Thank you to Sharia for helping us understand where our guides get the data we need, and another big thank you to Sharia for sharing this knowledge with us so we may go directly to it in the future."

I instructed Thea to take a few deep breaths, open her eyes, and come back to the present when she was ready.

"So, can you tell me what you experienced?" I asked her.

She slowly explained what she had witnessed during her meditation. Though many of the specifics were different (sizes, shapes, and colors) the basic gist was the same as what I experienced. She discovered, for the first time, that her guide, Sharia, was not even present during her psychic journey. Though she was asking for her guidance, she realized none of the metaphysical beings she saw were Sharia. She still felt amazingly comforted and even confident with what she was doing. She knew, now, that she would be able to connect to the universal energy she had perceived herself, without having to depend upon her guide.

While guides play an important role in connecting us to our intuition, we don't always have to resort to their energy to use our extrasensory gifts. Asking them for help is always okay, but not having to depend on them, rather being able to tune in ourselves, can prove to be even more powerful.

EXERCISE
. . . .
Go Deeper with Your Guide

Go somewhere quiet where you can relax and be uninter-
rupted. Using the same basic narrative I used in the story
with Thea and Sharia, begin your journey with, and without, your guides. Allow them to bring you to the place
where the information from the universe is imparted. Take
your time; this is an important step in increasing your psychic confidence.

Pay close attention to the details of where you metaphysically go. Look for any sentient beings or other objects
or items. Also, discern any colors that are present. Notice
if any of your previously discovered guides are there. Feel
whether you are familiar, comfortable, or distressed by
what you sense.

It's possible the scene may begin to fade as it did in my
meditation with Thea. But, if not, when you've gathered
every element about this metaphysical place, including
any new impressions about where psychic information
comes from, you can thank the universe and your guides
for bringing you on this journey. Either way, you are ready
to close it down. You might experience a slight sense of
sadness as where you just traveled metaphysically may
have brought about a feeling of bliss. This is actually very
common and is quite all right. Know you can visit again.
. . . .

You've discovered how to work with your guides on a more advanced level and you've learned where you can get the information from directly. You should be able to acquire psychic knowl-

edge with greater ease and more proficiency. You will find using your guides and their metaphysical location as a tool to access the data you need will help you to go deeper with your gifts. As always, act with an attitude of gratitude and be thankful for their guidance.

Increase Your Psychic Range with Psychometry

Psychometry is reading the energy of an object, as all objects and pictures hold energy. Psychometry is unique in that it allows you to gain knowledge from an item about the previous or current owner, their loved ones, deceased or living, and just about everything else about their personalities, careers, loves, desires, hopes, and even fears. Essentially, psychometry is perceiving information from an object using all your psychic abilities to connect to that data.

While practicing psychometry is a great beginning exercise, it can also take you to another level. It provides us with something tangible to help us connect to the energy of the person or even the object we are reading. Think of psychometry as a tool to be utilized to increase your range. It is a simple way to tap into your abilities and a great way to take them to the next level. We use our extrasensory perception to tune in to the owner's past, present, or their future. We also use it to access the object's history—where it came from, what it means, who may have owned it before, and what, if anything, is special about it. It is precisely because of the abundance of insight psychometry provides that makes this particular practice a great way to go beyond a beginner level reading.

It's not like you'll move right to intermediate- or expert-level readings with psychometry; expanding beyond a novice level isn't something you just jump into. It's more like a natural progression. Being aware of what you can already do will help you go further. Doing what you already can will start the process of going past what you've done before. By working with psychometry, you will harness and progress your psychic abilities.

Using psychometry as a tool forces you to focus by touching the object. Attaching yourself to the energy of the object provides you with an extension of the owner's energy. It also gives you a link to the energy of any of the people, places, or times involved with the object. To put it plainly, without psychometry it may feel like you have to filter out all the static from the universe when trying to hone in on psychic information. With psychometry, you still connect to the energy of the universe, but you have a focal point or dedicated line to receive the data you are asking for. Using this tool can help you cut through the chatter. It broadens your abilities, while at the same time, narrowing your search area.

Psychometry will provide you with the same types of impressions you would receive when working without it, but in a more direct way. Psychometry itself won't make you a better psychic. It will help you more easily gain access to information you might be trying to discern. You can think of it like using the internet; when you enter something into the search engine, you won't automatically become smarter, but you will be presented with the data you can use to increase your wisdom.

Perceiving psychic material via touch can also be accomplished by merely holding someone's hand. It works in the same basic manner as object psychometry, but some people feel it gives them a better pipeline to the information they are trying to tune in to. Often psychics will ask to hold their client's hand because it helps them to get into their sitter's energy more quickly, especially if they are only doing a short reading.

Many years ago, I was doing a quick, off-the-cuff reading for Tina, who was wondering about her new relationship. To help me get tuned in, I briefly held her hand and asked to hold her bracelet. When I touched her hand I immediately felt the love they had for each other and knew they had a real connection; I felt happy for them. When I held the bracelet I began seeing images, psychically in my mind's eye, which I presented to her.

"Have you ever been to Paris?" I asked.

"I've been there a few times," Tina responded.

"But, have you ever been there with Brian?" I continued.

"No … but we were talking about it," she answered, questioning.

I went on to explain that I saw the Eifel Tower and all the fairy-tale aspects of a romantic trip to France. I shared that this would, indeed, be a good relationship to invest her time and energy into. I also saw her beau on bended knee, proposing in front of the Eifel Tower, but I decided to keep that to myself to let her be surprised. Sure enough, Tina contacted me a couple of years later, confirming what I had seen in my vision. They invited me to their wedding!

Like all psychic tools, psychometry is available to enhance your psychic gifts, allowing for a better connection to the person you are trying to read. It will help you take your abilities to a level beyond beginner.

EXERCISE

· ·

Using Psychometry

For this exercise you will need some people to join you. Gather your friends and ask them to bring a few different objects (in a bag) they'd like to have read. Make sure they don't show anyone what they have; you don't want to see the objects. When everyone is ready, have them sit in a circle. Place your chair facing outward while the others face in. Place a pad and pen in your lap, ready to use.

Now, close your eyes. Breathe deeply until you feel relaxed. This is to be a blind reading; you are not to look at any of the items your group brought. Have your friends silently decide who will place one of their objects in your hand first.

As you inhale, imagine a silver funnel rising from the top of your head, reaching toward the sky. Feel it grow, stretch, and pulsate with energy. You may feel a tingling sensation on your scalp. Now, imagine beautiful, leafy vines coming out from the bottoms of your feet, grounding you down into the earth. Feel the healing energy as it runs back up into your feet and legs. Let this energy continue to move up, into your hips and abdomen, while letting the energy from the universe travel down through the funnel, into your head, through your shoulders and chest. Allow the energies to combine and continue traveling through your entire body.

Breathe deeply again. While your eyes remain closed, have the person previously designated place their item in your hand before quietly sitting back down. It is not important to try to figure out what the object is. As a matter of fact, you don't want to know what it is, as that may sway your thoughts.

As you hold the item in your hand, ask the universe to send information about the object through the silver funnel, down into your crown chakra. Without looking at the object (put it under your chair or hold it off to the side) write down all the impressions you receive on your pad, regardless of what they are and how they come to you. Do not censor it, record everything. Remember, just because what you perceive may not mean anything to you personally does not mean you should discount it—the information is not coming through for you. It is for whoever brought the object.

When you've finished writing down what your psychic senses have given you, it's time to go back and ask the object what else it has to tell you. Do not look at the object. Open your funnel even wider, with the intention of receiving even more information from the item. The impressions you've already recorded are what is immediately available to you. By increasing your funnel size, you are asking the universe to give you more. Again, write down whatever information you get now, using all your psychic abilities. When you've exhausted the messages you perceive, it's time to go deeper. You are no longer a beginner, and there is so much more you can gain. Ask for more by requesting the following specifics:

- Show me more, using my clairvoyance

- Tell me more, using my clairaudience

- Send me feelings, using my clairsentience

- Tell me something more, using my claircognizance

- Send me flavors, using my clairgustance

- Send me scents, using my clairalience

Write everything down. When you are finished recording, increase your funnel size again and answer the following:

- What colors do you see?

- What sounds do you hear?

- Do you get any specific locations? House, store, building, street, landscape, state, country?

- What do you get for time frames? Do you get any dates? Months? Years?

- How about names or initials? Do any stand out for you?

- Is the person who gave you the object the only owner? If not, whose was this or is this? Are they living or dead?

- If this is not the original owner, how are they connected to previous owners?

- How did the person who gave you the object obtain it?

- Are there any hobbies or professions connected to the object?

- Does the object feel positive or negative or neutral?

- Is the current owner happy? Sad? Angry? Excited? Depressed? Content? Afraid?
- Are there any messages, advice, or specific words that need to be shared?

When you are all done recording, open your funnel even bigger for the final time. This is your chance to really move beyond a beginner's level. Ask if there is anything else you can learn from the object you hold. Sense any vibrations through your hands and into your body. Tune in to the physical body and aura of the owner and note whether you feel anything off, like ailments or weaknesses. If you sense any physical issues, dive deeper and see if you perceive causes or treatments for them. Write down whatever impressions you receive. When you finish, open your eyes and turn your chair around.

Present your pad full of impressions to your friends. Be sure to tell them everything, without judgment, and let them tell you what makes sense and what doesn't. Suggest they keep an open mind and not write things off because they don't immediately click with them and take the messages to ponder them later. More often than not, people will connect with the messages shortly after they receive them.

After you've shared everything you wrote down, expand on your reading and let them know of any other impressions you had or are having that you didn't write down. Be sure to include any emotions or feelings you had that may not have been yours.

How did you do? Did you get more than 75 percent of the information validated? More than 50 percent? Less than that? Less than 25 percent? If you did very well, congratulate yourself! If you didn't, analyze what information you got wrong. Was it the initial data? Was it when you started asking specific questions? Was it after? Did you excel at a specific time during the exercise or was it scattered? Think of some of the topics we covered earlier. Were you caught in any negative thoughts? Was your ego blocking you?

Try it again. Shake your hands out, spin around, shake out your legs, and so on, to help clear the energy from the previous reading. Then, go through the entire process from the beginning with someone else's object. When you are done, compare them. Did you do better with one over the other? Did you find one easier? Were you able to connect to one person's energy more than another? Think about how this practice made you feel. Did you like psychometry? Did it bring you further than you'd been before? Do you feel like you connected on a deeper level?

. . . .

Psychometry is one way to access your psychic abilities. You can go into it as deep as your gifts allow you. Pushing your boundaries in ways you've never tried before will aid in the development of your intuition and expand your psychic aptitude. Holding an object, like jewelry, a photograph, or another item, provides you with an advantage. You have instant access through touch to the owner's energy, which can make it easier to go beyond your beginning level.

While using tools is not a necessity when increasing your gifts, it is a smart move. When choosing to develop anything in life, it is always prudent to take advantage of everything there is to increase your knowledge. Using psychic tools can get you past that stalled-out point, where you feel like you are not getting any better. Guides, though referred to in many ways like helpers, can be one of your most valuable tools. But like psychometry to other forms of tools (tarot or oracle cards, crystals, tea leaves), they should not be used solely as a crutch. You can depend on your gifts to tune in to the metaphysical and utilize the tools to give you a broader, yet more focused and stronger connection. This connection can be deepened to help you connect to the other side, to deceased loved ones and those that have passed.

CHAPTER 6

....

Mediumship

Connecting to the other side, becoming the medium for someone who has passed on or died a physical death, is not an automatically guaranteed skill when developing your psychic gifts. There are some people who are natural mediums, meaning they are born with the ability to talk to those who have transitioned on, and usually can do it for themselves as well as others. For the most part, though, when attempting to increase your psychic gifts you may find you have to practice connecting. If you've discovered you have a strong aptitude working with energy, there is a high probability you are already channeling information, possibly without being aware of it. Mediumship is, at its core, the channeling of messages and data from the other side.

How to Connect

Connecting to deceased loved ones on the other side is similar to connecting to our guides, but usually, if we are doing it for someone else, we have no personal bond to them. While we may have a relationship with our client or the sitter we are reading for, that's probably where the union ends. This, I have found, can often make it easier to get a pure connection to the dead we are trying to bring through because we have no preconceived notions about them and no idea who they were when they were alive. If we know the person who passed or information about them, it can be more difficult or you may pull through information that's tainted with your own judgments or feelings toward that deceased person. We tend to try to rationalize what they'd want to share or what kind of person they were. Not knowing them allows an unadulterated reading.

One key ingredient to tuning in to the dead is to be open to speaking with whoever is coming through. Now, this must have limits, of course. When communicating with the other side, you want to be sure you speak with positive spirits, letting nothing with harmful or negative intentions come through. Usually you can accomplish this by simply stating your intentions. If you still feel there is negative energy, tell it to go away. Say it in your mind but also aloud. Let the energy know you will not, in any way, entertain it and you won't communicate with them. Order them to leave. However, if you are trying to connect to someone else's deceased loved ones, it is possible that negative entity is there for them. Ask. They may have been negative or had negative energy around them when they were alive, so that may be how they show up. Be direct that you will only speak to them if they show up without the intent to harm you or the person you are reading for. Clear of any toxic energies, you are free to open your psychic senses to receive messages from your clients' deceased loved ones or your dead loved ones.

Another significant ingredient to mediumship is to allow that we don't always know how we are going to connect. We can create the space for them to come through, as in during a reading, but it doesn't dictate how they will show up. I've had many people come through in many different and unexpected ways. Some people will immediately share how they died and some will tell me their name or their initial. Other times the person coming through will share something about their life before they passed, or they will communicate something about the person they are there for. And, yet still, they might show up with a random reference that's difficult to immediately recognize.

I was at Barnes & Noble doing a book event and the audience was fantastic! Rather than just doing a signing, we practiced using our abilities during a workshop. Everyone participated, and we had a great time. The thing that perplexed me was no one asked about their dead people. This was unheard of! I mean, honestly, if I had a psychic medium on stage who was taking questions, I would absolutely ask if any of my peeps were there. But, this group was very polite.

"Okay. Does anyone have any final questions before we wrap this up?" I asked them.

They proceeded to ask me questions about tuning in to their psychic gifts. I answered them and then asked, "I can't believe none of you are going to ask me if your loved ones are here. Don't you want to know?" I chuckled.

Immediately people started asking about their relatives, after explaining, "We didn't want to bother you or be rude!"

They were so concerned with not bothering me that they didn't inquire about their loved ones, but the loved ones weren't so worried about it! They wanted to come through.

The first question I got was simple, "Who, if anyone, is here for me?"

I answered the audience and brought through a bunch of people they were able to recognize. Although every dead person is different, mostly they come through with simple messages of love or something to let their loved ones know they are around. Up to this point, this time was no different. Then, I tasted something strange.

"Sour cream? Does anyone have a connection to sour cream?" I asked, incredulously. I could taste it on my lips. Then I heard the actual words: *sour cream*.

"Nope. No. Not that I know of!" I heard in response. I kept trying.

"Hmmm, could it be cream cheese? Did someone have nachos before they came? Or Mexican food? I can't really think of anything else. I think it's sour cream, though ... I can taste it!" I continued, with a grin. "I know it doesn't make much sense, but I feel like sour cream is significant."

The group just laughed—no one claimed the message.

I said to them, "That's okay. Just take it with you. Hopefully, someone will get it, eventually! Either that or it is a premonition that we should have some yummy Mexican food for dinner!"

We giggled a bit at my expense and wrapped up the event. I began signing books and card decks that people were purchasing. As we worked through the line, my patrons asked more questions and we had discussions about how their personal psychic abilities were showing up. As we talked, I noticed a woman hanging back. I could tell she wanted to talk alone.

When all the others left, she came up with her friend to have their books signed.

"Hi! Did you enjoy the seminar?" I asked them both.

"Yes, very much!" they agreed, unanimously.

"That's great. I'm glad! So ... what's going on?" I knew she had something to say.

The woman gave me a nervous laugh and said, "I just wanted to tell you I figured out what you were talking about."

As she told me her eyes welled up.

"Oh, good. Do tell."

"My granddaughter died recently. Toward the end of her life she couldn't eat anything, so we put sour cream inside her lips so she could at least taste something. I can't believe I didn't realize what you were talking about," she said, teary-eyed.

"Yes, you did, it just took a couple of minutes. Your granddaughter was letting you know she is around and she appreciated what you did to help make her last days better," I shared with her.

Suffering a loss like that is never easy, but knowing they are never far helps, as it did for this grieving grandmother. None of us want to sever our connections to our loved ones. We crave them. We need them. We want to know they are around. That is why some people will do just about anything to keep their bond alive. Top on the list? They will go to see a medium and hope the psychic can bring them through.

Connecting to the other side, and more specifically to a person on the other side, can be tricky but it can be developed. An important thing to remember is trying to force it won't make it happen. Practicing silencing your mind will help you more than trying to will it to happen. Quieting your thoughts and bonding with your own spirit are prerequisites to being able to connect to someone else's spirit. Learning to differentiate between your chatter and messages from the deceased will support your quest for advancing your psychic skills, and stilling your mind can be the beginning.

EXERCISE
. . . .

Silence Your Mind and Connect to Spirit

Meditating to silence the mind is not always difficult, but creating a stillness while remaining open to spiritual contact can be tougher. To begin, go somewhere you won't be disturbed for at least a half hour and bring your journal. Make sure there are no noises, such as music, ringing phones, or barking dogs. Once there, lie down and get comfortable.

Close your eyes and breathe deeply. Focus on your breath. Feel the air as it travels in through your nose. Hold your breath before exhaling and feel the oxygen as it travels through your torso and down your limbs. When you breathe out, notice how your head and face feel. Continue breathing, in and out, concentrating on how your body feels as you do.

Now, listen. Listen with your ears, and with your body. Hear any noises and release them. Feel any physical vibrations with your body and let them go. Listen to your surroundings, hear every sound there is, and then free yourself from it by quieting your mind even more. Liberate yourself from every external sound and vibration. Inhale deeply again, and listen to how it sounds, what you hear as you exhale. Keep breathing until you hear nothing but your breath.

Now, listen inside your mind, listen to the silence. Let every thought escape, leaving only stillness. Inhale again and listen as the oxygen mingles with your blood cells, traveling throughout your body, and into your face and head. Exhale and feel the silence surround you. Let go of your conscious thought. Remain here until you are content in the stillness of your mind and body.

Then, when you are ready, breathe again. Imagine you have antennae curling out of your head. These antennae reach out to connect to the energy on the other side. You can tune the antennae like you can tune a radio. Go ahead and tune the antennae to connect to the other side. You can fine-tune them as needed.

Now that you know what stillness sounds like and feels like in your mind, listen for spirit. Continue breathing and on the exhale pay specific attention to any sounds you hear other than your own breath. Ask for someone from the other side, with the highest intentions, to send you a message or a thought. You can ask who it is, but it's more important to ask for a simple sign that they are there. Let them share with you, don't force it. You want the message to be pure. Listen. Feel.

Breathe in again and listen. Exhale and fine-tune your antennae. Ask for more. Be ready to listen to whatever messages, sounds, or feelings come through. Then, do it again. Keep doing it until you are sure it is not your own thoughts or imaginings that you perceive. Breathe again. Stay in this space, linked to the other side for as long as you are comfortable.

Once you are done, turn off the antennae, coiling them back up until you're ready to use them again. Come back to the quiet of your own mind. Relish in the stillness for a bit and enjoy the peace and solitude. When you are ready, take another breath and open your eyes. Grab your journal and record anything you received, even if you're not sure what it was or what it meant or even if you think it was your imagination. If you didn't receive anything, do you think it was because you couldn't quiet your mind enough? If so, keep practicing. This may take some time to accomplish.

• •

We are constantly distracted by so much. With the chaos of life and the cacophony of sound around us, it can be very difficult to tune in to the other side. Creating a still and relaxed state makes it easier to cross the barrier. Don't be discouraged if you had a hard time working the exercise. You can repeat the lessons as often as you'd like.

Intuiting Evidence

To be sure you are indeed connecting to deceased loved ones of the person you are reading for, you need to provide evidence. This is not necessary to determine your truth or whether you are intentionally lying. There are no medium police. Rather, it helps to increase your self-confidence and the belief that you are actually doing it. It also provides your sitter with the proof they need to feel the bond with their loved ones. Evidence can be initials or names, something they were recognized for, or a special thing that makes your sitter say, "Wow! How could you possibly have known that?" There are no set rules about what the evidence is, but you want to receive it and present it as clearly as possible.

Getting the evidence you're looking for is not always possible, however to be sure you are really bringing through someone's grandmother you must be able to tell them more than just, "She loves you." This, though it may be true, is way too generic. You need evidence to demonstrate to your client and yourself that the person you're linking to is who you think it is. I am not one to prove to anyone that psychic ability is real just because they are challenging me, but if you are doing a reading, you do need to substantiate that you have a true connection.

I was teaching a webinar recently with my sister. It was about using intuition to empower yourself. Toward the end of the seminar we asked for questions. Ronette asked a common question. "What does my grandmother want me to know?"

Immediately I saw a fleeting image of a car. Then I saw an image of a fence. I got distracted for a moment while teaching because many questions were asked at once by multiple students. But when it came back around I told Ronette about the fence.

"Does that mean anything to you? Is it something personal? If you don't understand the fence as literal, it may be symbolic."

I waited to see if she wrote anything in the online chat room of the webinar. Nothing. I continued with the reading, intuitively knowing there was something to it.

"Symbolically, fences are either barriers to something or are about making the decision to jump. In other words, choosing which way to go. In your case, I do feel like you're in the middle of trying to make a lot, and I mean a lot, of decisions. I feel like your grandmother was there for the fence and she is there to help you with all your decisions. She is telling you to trust your intuition. Your instincts about the fence were also right. She said she helped you. She is still helping you with the choices you need to make—you need only ask her. But, she reiterated that she helped you with the fence!" I told her.

She didn't seem to connect right away, but then I saw she wrote she was dealing with a lot of decisions.

"I do have a lot going on right now. I'm in the middle of a bunch of things I need to decide on and I'm having a hard time. I'm glad my grandmother is there to help me!" she wrote.

"Great! But, hold on to the fence thing. I have a feeling you will understand more about the fence later," I assured her.

We continued the seminar and closed it down. A couple of hours later I received an e-mail from Ronette.

"Melanie, I just have to tell you I figured out what the fence was about! Yesterday, I pulled into work, parked my car, and went inside. I must have left my manual car in neutral without the emergency brake on and it rolled backward, through the parking lot, took a turn, and crashed into a fence. It didn't really hurt anything, just a scratch, and it avoided all the other cars. It is almost impossible for my car to have ended up hitting the fence the way it did. It was like someone was driving it in reverse through the parking lot and then took a sharp turn into the fence. My daughter saw it yesterday and said how the heck did it not just roll straight backward and hit a group of mailboxes. My boss stated after it happened that it appeared as if an angel was behind the wheel of my car."

Wow, and her grandmother had said she was there, helping her with the fence situation. So, as frequently happens, the fence played a double role for Ronette's reading. It was literal, and it was symbolic. I tell my students and clients all the time to look at both meanings in readings as we don't want to discount one or neglect one for the other. Ronette was right in the middle of a bunch of life-changing decisions, and her car had literally hit a fence. This, along with a few other things more specific to her grandmother, like her incredible age (she was 112 when she passed!) and her very strong personality, was evidence that she really had come through.

There are many ways to offer evidence. The aha moment is big, and that usually causes the person you're reading for to open wide and acknowledge many other things you may bring that otherwise might have been overlooked. For example, imagine Sam came in for a reading. Before telling Sam that his brother Charlie was there in spirit, you talked about Fords and granola. It meant nothing to Sam, but it's what his brother had driven and eaten for breakfast every morning when he was alive. When you then told Sam his brother was here, he was able to connect to the messages—they were evidence of Charlie being there. Expect to get evidence, because you can ask for it. Don't demand it—solicit it; request it.

EXERCISE
· ·
Asking for Evidence

Find a friend or even a stranger who wants to connect to someone who has passed, but don't let them tell you anything about anyone you may connect with. Ask that someone come through who was a friend or loved one, so you can validate your information after your exercise, preferably with information you wouldn't know. You want to be somewhere you can relax and have some privacy and quiet for a bit of time. Make sure you bring your journal; you will need to write your evidence down. Before you begin, set the intention that no harmful or dangerous spirits can come to you, only those who are helpful and optimistic, filled with constructive and encouraging messages.

As always, get comfortable and breathe deeply. Close your eyes when you are ready. Continue relaxing, inhaling positive energy, exhaling anything that no longer belongs to you. Feel the energy of your breath traveling through your body, creating a tranquil response, calming you.

Now imagine you're standing in the woods with the sunlight dappling through the trees, reaching down to send you light. You can feel the warm leaves and the moss under your feet. The earth is reaching up sending you energy to connect you to the universe. As you take a step, you feel the light fill you up. Keep walking; as your feet touch down each time, you receive more light flowing through you. As you look down at your hands, you see them glowing, illuminated with energy.

There is an opening to a cave in front of you. There is green grass all around the opening, and flowers emerging from the earth. The cave beckons you with healing energy. Step inside and sit down on the ground, feeling the dry dirt underneath you. Place your palms facedown, and feel the vibrations of the earth. Look up to the top of the cave and see an opening directly above you that reaches all the way to the sky and beyond.

Imagine the top of your head, your crown chakra, opening wide, ready to connect to the other side. Feel the pulse of the universe as you tap into the energy of the deceased. The cave is there to keep you safe and to bring the energy in through the opening, straight down to you. Only those with the most affirming and helpful intentions can come through. Reach up with your mind and call in a soul from the other side that wants to share a message through you for your sitter. When you feel like you have a connection to someone, you can begin asking the following questions:

- How old were they when they passed? If you don't get a distinct answer, you can ask for a decade (i.e., 1–10, 10–20, 20–30, and so on).
- Were they male or female?
- What did they look like? Did they have any distinguishing features like tattoos or birthmarks?
- Were they a friend or a relative of the person they are bringing messages for?

- How did they die? Was it a quick or a slow death? A natural death or an accident or even a murder? An expected death or a surprise?

- What did they do when they were alive? Did they work? Student? Retired?

- Did they have any hobbies?

- Were they known for something specific?

- What is a specific memory they share with your sitter?

- What is something they can share with you that happened in your sitter's life after their passing?

- Is there anyone else on the other side that is connected to your sitter, including pets as well as people that have passed? Was anyone there to greet them when they crossed over or have they greeted anyone who has passed since?

- Why did they come through? Is there a specific reason?

- Do they come through often?

- Do they have a message to give the sitter?

- Do they have a message for you?

- Is there anything else they want to share?

Finally, thank the deceased for coming through.

When you are all done asking the questions, take a deep breath and open your eyes. Did you get answers to your questions? Write down everything you received, and then record any additional intuitive feelings, thoughts, or visions you had. Discuss all the information you received with your sitter. Remember, don't leave anything out or discount anything—it's not for you, it's for them. Go through your entire list before they respond to you. Make sure they are wide open to receiving messages from even unexpected sources.

How did it feel to connect? Did you feel like it was your imagination? Did you feel confident that you were connecting to the other side? Did you get enough detailed evidence to relay to your sitter? Are they able to validate the information you received? Do they know who it was that came through? Did you receive any specific messages?

Having these questions helps you to access information. This list can be used to facilitate your connection to the other side each time you do mediumship. Requesting the particulars allows you to gain the evidence you need to confirm you are truly linked in. Leaving it open to receive a link to anyone connected to your sitter can sometimes make it easier to tune in to someone. Having a certain person to connect with sets your intention more specifically, but will not always work.

Transfiguration in Mediumship

Transfiguration is an interesting form of mediumship. Essentially, it is a visual metamorphosis of the face of the medium or sitter into their spirit guide or a deceased spirit. It is a way to recognize who is coming through. This is accomplished by using spirit energy or ectoplasm, which is a spirit energy you can see, sometimes in the form of mist or something thicker. You may have heard of this in the movie *Ghostbusters*, in which they trapped the ectoplasmic ghosts in their machines. Even though this was a comedy, it had a basis in truth. Diana Palm, medium and author who practiced and witnessed transfiguration at Arthur Findlay College in England with physical and trance mediums, shares in her book, "Transfiguration occurs when a trance medium raises their vibration and allows spirit to draw ectoplasm from their body to show themselves in a mist-like substance in front of them. Ectoplasm is something all living beings have and it has been referred to as spiritual energy."[8] Physical mediums allow a spirit to manipulate their energy and the energy of physical objects to come through.

Many mediums will use transfiguration to physically show their sitters or their audience who is coming through. Others, like myself, will view the guides and deceased loved ones on the face of their sitter. This is what happened the first time I ever used transfiguration in one of my client sessions.

Phoenix had come in for a reading. The session was a normal session and I received messages in the way I was used to. All my psychic senses were employed to give her the information from the other side. After discussing her past, present, and future, she was interested in connecting to whoever wanted to come through. So, I asked my guides to bring her spirits to the surface. Usually when I do this, I receive symbolic messages or a word or two that I share with my client that provides them with their aha moment. This is pretty normal in most readings. I give the evidence I receive to the sitter, but this time was different.

---

8. Palm, Diana. *Mediumship Scrying & Transfiguration for Beginners: A Guide to Spirit Communication*. Woodbury, MN: Llewellyn Publications, 2017.

"Okay, I'm going to try to connect specifically to your peeps on the other side," I told her, "though, as always, I'm not sure who will come through."

I looked at Phoenix as I asked to bring someone through for her, and I noticed her face changing. The more I stared at her, the more I noticed it transforming and physically changing her face, as though someone had overlaid a tight-fitting image upon her skin. This had never happened before during my sessions.

"I'm seeing an older woman, she looks to be Native American. She has long dark hair and a sharper, longer nose. Her skin is darker than yours, a dark tan, and I see she has a large turquoise necklace on. She has dark eyes with crinkles around them, otherwise known as laugh lines," I giggle.

I waited for an answer from her as I stared, somewhat mesmerized, at the face that had morphed over hers.

"Wow, I can't say that we have any Native Americans in our family. I've never heard of that lineage in our family tree at all, as a matter of fact," she responded, kind of disappointed.

As she spoke I could see the face of the woman still superimposed on hers.

"I know many people have Native American guides, but I don't think that's who this is. I believe it's your relative, a couple of generations back. She is not really telling me anything other than she wants you to know she is with you and can help you in some way," I tell her.

"All right, though I don't really think she's here for me. Or maybe she's my guide and not a relative. Maybe you're just getting it mixed up," she replied, in a nice but definitive way.

"Well, I've been off before. After all, this is not an exact science. Hold on to it and take it with you. I think you'll figure it out eventually," I counter as my client's face reappears and the Native American woman slowly dissipates.

I know what I saw, and I could have been wrong, but I didn't think so. I did the best I could and decided to let the universe sort the rest out. If it was important, Phoenix would discover it—or not. Either way, I knew I saw something amazing during that session. The woman was real, of that I was certain. We would have to see how she was connected to Phoenix.

The next day I received an e-mail from my client. She had relayed the information about the reading to her mom and asked if they had a Native American connection. Her mother told Phoenix that this was a huge revelation. Generations back, there had been rumors that Phoenix's great-great-great-grandfather had an affair with a Native American woman. Everyone denied it. Soon, he had a daughter with his wife. But, the family secret was that the Native American woman died during childbirth and the baby was adopted by Phoenix's non-biological great-great-great-grandmother. No one ever knew it wasn't hers. The woman who showed up in Phoenix's reading turned out to be her Native American biological great-great-great-grandmother, which also explained Phoenix's baby boy's darker features.

This session turned out to be an incredible turning point for me. Having the ability to recognize transfiguration opened another technique to be used in both psychic readings and mediumship. Once you recognize this is possible, it allows you to access the deceased in a whole new way.

Phoenix was not aware that her deceased relative had used her face to help me. She played no conscious part in the transformation, but it allowed me to see her relative in a different way. Sometimes, transfiguration will occur this way, where the sitter has no idea it is happening. Other times they can, with intent, allow their relatives to use them to aid in recognition. Also, the medium can offer their own faces to be used to help their clients physically see their deceased loved ones by allowing them to superficially impose their image upon the psychic.

EXERCISE
. . . .
Medium Transfiguration

For this exercise you will need a partner. Try to find someone or a group with the same curiosity as you, who wants to expand their mediumistic abilities. Get together and form a circle. You will be the medium first. As the medium, you will allow the transfiguration to occur on your face. After that, the sitter(s) will have their own guides and loved ones transform their faces. (Another way to practice is to use a mirror. This is a great option if you don't have a partner or if you want to try to call in your own deceased loved ones.) Dim the lighting in the room. If it's convenient, turn off the lights and use candles. Sometimes this makes it easier to view the metamorphic changes.

Have everyone relax, close their eyes, and call their loved ones in. Ask that only positive energies come forward. When you are ready, you can begin. As the medium, you will be channeling the energies and allowing them to use your physical body to show themselves. This may be somewhat draining, so it's important for you to breathe deeply to keep the oxygen flowing. Open your chakras and feel your spirit reach out to the other side, calling forth the spirits of those connected to your guests. Relax yourself and close your eyes. Inhale and imagine you're in an art classroom. All around you are your sitters, your audience. When you feel comfortable, say these words out loud:

"I am here to act as a channel for the deceased loved ones of my audience to come through. Please, one at a time, use my face as your canvas and allow my audience to help bring you through. I am opening myself for you to alter my physical appearance temporarily, so my sitters may view you and recognize who you are and who you were when you were alive. Please, gently transform me now, one soul at a time. Thank you for allowing me to share your messages as well."

Now relax and open your eyes. Imagine you are painted by the loved one coming through. Feel their energy on your face and ask if they have any messages for their loved ones. Also ask for a name or an initial to share with your audience to help them recognize the spirit who has superimposed their features onto your face. Look to your audience and share whatever information you have. Ask them if they recognize the messages you bring through and ask if they recognize your face.

Take turns bringing through as many deceased loved ones as you have sitters by allowing them to paint their faces on yours. When you are done and have shared all their messages, it is time to switch roles. While still acting as the medium, ask that they come through and appear on their loved ones' faces. Look to your audience, one by one, and see if you are able to witness their transfiguration. Then share what you view as well as any messages they share with you.

When you are done, have everyone take deep breaths and open their eyes if they are not yet open. Discuss, in depth, the messages that came through and the faces you saw. Was it easier to view the loved ones when they appeared on your face or on the sitters' faces? Was your group able to see faces on your face? Were they clear? How did it feel to allow spirit to distort and change your energy this way? How did it feel for your sitters?

. . . .

If you couldn't accomplish this, don't fret. This can be extremely difficult for some. It can be tough to channel someone to begin with, but to transform your faces can be even harder. Transfiguration, on the other hand, may prove to be one of your favorite ways to connect, especially if you are a natural clairvoyant. Either way, don't give up on this method of mediumship. Try it with other people, possibly one-on-one instead of with a group, or vice versa. Also, try it without a partner by using a mirror and allow your deceased loved ones to use your face as their canvas to show you they are there. As with any developing gift, it may not happen immediately—practice often, and you will find it will become easier.

Closing Your Psychic Gifts

Leaving yourself wide open to mediumship in any form when you are not specifically trying to communicate with the other side or working as a medium can establish a pattern that generates unwanted and untimely communications. Learning to close it down sufficiently is a significant part of doing mediumship. It's also a responsible part of tuning in to your psychic gifts. You don't want to allow just anyone or anything to come through when you are not tuned in. But, sometimes it does happen.

I was at an overnight goddess weekend event. There were a lot of women there and the following day I was scheduled to do about six hours of private readings. I was in bed, writing of course, and it was very late, about 2 a.m. I was sharing the room with two other women, and one of them, Lynn, was in bed already, like me. I was thinking about the readings I was going to be doing the next day and sending the universe a message that I wanted to be able to connect well.

All of a sudden, I started getting information. I didn't want to tune in then, and I didn't try to. I think my guides and Lynn's guides and loved ones had the bright idea to jump-start her reading.

"Lynn," I began.

"Yes, Melanie?" she responded. I had a feeling she knew what was coming. This wasn't the first time it had happened with Lynn. Her deceased loved ones had a habit of showing up.

"Okay, well here we go. I've got some people here for you … are you ready?" I asked her, already knowing her answer.

"Yes, of course I am!" she eagerly responded.

Lynn was used to this and was very open to receiving messages; in fact, she loved when this happened.

"Who are the *M* names?" I asked her. "These women are here for you."

"Both M's are my grandmothers. Anything else?" she replied, with total nonchalance.

"Well, I'm getting an *R* to go with it," I answered.

"Yup, that's Grandma Meredith's last name. Anyone else hanging out?"

I told her I was going to tell them to come back during her reading the following day, that I didn't want them to come to me now.

"Ugh. They're not going away. Who are all of the *S* and *C* names? There's like a total of six!" I continued. "Go to sleep, Lynn! Tell them to leave me alone—I have to write!" I joked.

"Hey, you're the one who's talking to them. And yes, there are four *S*s and two *C*s. You are right on," Lynn laughed.

"Ha! All right, go to sleep—now!"

"Okay, but I'm not the one calling them in!" she chuckled.

I was quiet for a minute, writing some more, trying to ignore the image I kept seeing. Finally, I couldn't hold back anymore.

"What's with the cowboys? Is someone a cowboy? Or do they wear a cowboy hat or boots or something?"

"Yup. Most of my family lives in Texas—they *are* cowboys," Lynn said, cracking up. "Now, *you* go to sleep!"

I laughingly told her we would have to wait and see whether anyone decided to come back through during her upcoming session. At that point I was able to shut it down by asking them to leave, and I turned off my computer and lay down.

In this instance, being open to her loved ones the night before the reading was something I created because I asked for a good connection during the sessions I was scheduled to do the following day, including one for Lynn. But, after joking with Lynn a bit, I was able to put them on hold until her official reading to come through. They listened and revisited us with even more messages. When you focus your intent on doing mediumship and working with your psychic abilities, you are vulnerable to visitations. If you feel overwhelmed, or like you are wide open, you can always shut it down. You don't want to close yourself off entirely, but you need to let the spiritual realm know they are not to come through unless you ask or if there are extraordinary circumstances.

EXERCISE
. . . .
Shut It Down

Go somewhere quiet. You need to shut down your link enough so you will stay protected but available at the same time. Take a few deep breaths to relax. Close your eyes and relax more deeply.

Imagine a big sunflower-like showerhead above your head, shining a brilliant and sparkly silver. Out of that showerhead comes a gentle but continuous energy rain. Now, think about how the energy flows in from the universe, through your crown chakra, down your body, getting interpreted and digested in all your chakras, and in the goosebumps along your body. This is how you connect to everyone—even the other side. You know it feels amazing; it is cleansing and exciting. Allowing this energy to flow through you and around you feels incredible, and you know you are at one with the universe. But, you are also getting information about situations, people, and those who've passed. If you let this continue unchecked, it will overwhelm you and take over your life.

There is a way to slow down the flow of information you receive. Just as you can open yourself to receiving more, you can reduce the stream so you can focus on your physical life, too, without being interrupted by spirit. Imagine reaching out to a shower knob in front of you. Turn it clockwise as far as it can go. This will open the valve and let the energy pour in and around you. Relish in this feeling for a moment. Pay attention to what it feels like, what it looks like, what it sounds like, and even what it tastes like. Notice anyone or anything that comes through, whether sharing a message or just goose bumps to make you aware of the energetic presence.

Now, turn the knob as far counterclockwise as you can. It may feel as though you just closed yourself off to the world, which essentially, you are doing. You might experience a sense of overwhelming isolation. When this feeling becomes too claustrophobic or too oppressive, reach out and turn the knob, slowly, clockwise again, until it feels comfortable. You want to find a good balance between allowing yourself to feel connected versus feeling overloaded.

It's up to you to choose how open you want your shower of energy to be. The more open, the more information will pour in. When you feel you've adjusted it to the ideal setting, open and closed just enough, you can take a deep breath and open your eyes.

• •

You can control the flow of information with this exercise. Use it whenever you feel you are too exposed or if you are having a hard time connecting. Often, the people you are with will automatically raise or lower your frequency which adjusts your flow. You'll have to tweak it to accommodate for their energy. Again, where you have your faucet set will not stay constant. You may find you need to modify your settings to adapt to your surroundings.

Not everyone who is psychic will be a medium, though all mediums are psychic. Being a medium requires you put aside any preconceived ideas of the person trying to come through, as well as the person you are reading for. If you are trying to connect for yourself, it may be a bit more difficult. Chances are you know the person you are trying to connect with and that alone can make it harder to avoid pulling from your memories. But, when you ask for evidence and you receive it in some way, you will know you are connecting. Knowing there are specific questions you can ask to help provide you that evidence you need is a prudent way to access that proof. Seeing someone's face morph into who you are trying to connect to can also be an amazing way to demonstrate who you are communicating with. Mediumship can be extremely draining, so you want to be able to slow the flow of information down and control when you are open to the other side. Protecting yourself allows you to sustain your energy when you are ready to connect. Knowing how to protect yourself will also help keep you safe while traveling through lifetimes.

CHAPTER 7
....
Gifts from the Past

Our mind, body, and spirit work together in a way that completes us as people. They are not the same, however. Each is a distinct part of us. Our minds can be exercised by learning and challenging our beliefs. We can increase our knowledge and brain power by learning, studying, and just living. Our body, too, can be physically exercised. We function better all-around when we treat our bodies with respect—eating right, sleeping enough, and exercising. Our spirits also need to be respected, as these, unlike our body, are ageless. We each are a spiritual being living in a physical body. Past-life expert Dr. Brian Weiss is an author and doctor who stumbled upon past-life regression as a means to bring healing and understanding to his patients. He writes, "Our bodies may be constrained by this physical dimension, but our minds and souls are not ... Our souls are as vast and limitless as the stars."[9] Our souls, our ageless spirits, are gifts that live on.

---

9. Weiss, Brian. *Miracles Happen: The Transformational Healing Power of Past-Life Memories.* New York: Harper Collins Publishers, 2012.

Bringing Gifts Forward from Past Lives

We are influenced by every different lifetime we've lived, and we can consciously pull abilities we've already developed from past lives. Knowing this adds a whole new dimension of possibility. Just imagine how amazing it would be to not have to start at square one. By bringing forward psychic talents you've cultivated in your past, you will find yourself further ahead than you may have thought. As with your five physical senses, your sixth sense will benefit from any lessons you've already studied. Think of yourself as a sponge that absorbs liquid. You've soaked up a variety of intuitive talents over the years that you can take advantage of now.

Tracy came in one day for a past-life regression. She was hoping to uncover something that would help explain her current-life issues. So, we brought her back for her first regression. She immediately connected to a Native American lifetime. (Though somewhat cliché, Native American lifetimes are very common.) Tracy explained in her session that she felt she was a man from the Iroquois tribe and there was someone from a warring tribe chasing him. She described the mask the enemy wore and talked about the year, the early 1700s. Alli, the name Tracy was called during her past life, spoke of traveling alone and having to protect himself from predators. Alli felt lonely and scared, often relying on his intuition to survive. In the end, he died by himself.

At the end of the session, I asked Alli what he needed to share with Tracy, what she could let go of in this lifetime, and what lesson she no longer needed. He told her she needn't be alone anymore and that she didn't have to be afraid or hide because there were no predators in her current lifetime.

Tracy revealed that she currently, in this lifetime, had almost a dozen children and lived in a remote wooded area, but with her family around her she no longer felt lonely. She was able to relax a bit, and not be afraid because Alli had confirmed she was not being hunted. She e-mailed me after the session to validate that the Native American who was chasing Alli was indeed part of the Mohawk tribe and all the names and dates corresponded to the evidential data she researched afterward. She was able to find the name Alli, short for Alliquippa, was indeed an Iroquois name. Being able to confirm the information she was given from her previous life helped her understand the lessons she brought forward, as well as the knowledge that came with it.

Past Lives and Their Influences

Our spirit is stronger and more resilient than our physical body, so we live on after our physical body dies. We learn through every lifetime and to some extent we retain much of the knowledge we've garnered, in our spiritual body. This wisdom can be utilized in your present life to help you expand your psychic awareness. Your past lives can also influence your beliefs and your gifts in this lifetime. They often affect what you are afraid of and how you react to things in the present, including how deeply you go into the metaphysical realm.

As a psychic, I don't like to tell people who they were in previous lifetimes. Rather, I like them to discover it for themselves through past-life regression. What I do know is everyone who has regressed with me discovers at least one past life and associates that life on multiple levels to this lifetime. Often, they are surprised by what they did, but they can usually relate it to their actions now. This goes for psychic gifts as well. I've worked with some clients who have come out of their regression with their metaphysical abilities stronger than they were before.

Jan, a twenty-year-old, came into my office wanting to explore her intuition and to learn how to tap into and expand her natural psychic ability.

"We can approach this in a couple of different ways," I told her. "I can mentor you and we can work on developing your gifts. Or, we can try doing a past-life regression and pull some of your previous abilities into this lifetime to increase what you're already working with. What do you think?"

"Wow, I hadn't considered that," Jan replied. "Do you think that would help?"

"There's only one way to see," I told her.

We began the past-life regression and almost immediately Jan was transported back to a recent lifetime, in the 1940s, where she discovered she was a healer. She was able to work with people using her medical intuition and practiced hands-on healing or laying-on of hands. But, that wasn't all. She immediately jumped back to another lifetime.

She discovered she was a healer, and a witch. She was able to psychically see things for people. She felt afraid of her gifts, though. She hid them, so she wouldn't be persecuted or even tortured or killed for it. She was afraid for her life, so she learned to not expose who she was and what she was capable of. She kept that she could view the future to herself. She was more comfortable healing or helping to heal others, though she never shared how she did it.

When Jan was done exploring these two lifetimes, I brought her back to the present. As she came back through the years, we asked her guides and her higher self to allow her gifts to come back with her. When she opened her eyes, there was a spark that hadn't been there before. Right away she began talking, very animatedly.

"I was a witch! I hid my power, my psychic abilities! That makes perfect sense. That's why I feel like I'm clairvoyant, but it always seems just out of reach. I also knew I was a healer. That's why I've wanted to change my major to nursing. Wow, this is so exciting!" she exclaimed.

I told her to be with this new energy for a while and practice her psychic exercises. When she called me a week later her excitement was still palpable.

"I can't believe it. I can see. My clairvoyant gifts are opening more than I can remember they ever did before. Also, I'm surprised by my medical intuitive abilities now. I can see inside a person's energy and figure out where they're blocked or if they have a health issue. This is amazing," Jan said, and I knew it was just the beginning for her.

When I facilitated Jan's past-life regression, it was as though she went back in time and was able to pull forward her psychic gifts that had lain dormant during this lifetime. She was able to assimilate her past-life gifts with her current life. But, what was almost more interesting was that she knew there was something currently missing, she just couldn't figure out exactly what it was. Traveling back in time had allowed her to discover what she didn't know she had forgotten. Luckily, she found it again, and so can you!

Past-life regression is a form of hypnosis. Generally, a good hypnotist, someone specifically trained to facilitate past-life regressions, can bring you back to a place and time where you lived before: same soul, different body. But, having someone like me, a certified hypnotist trained and certified in past-life regression and a practicing psychic, is the perfect blend to help you go back in order to bring forward your own abilities. However, past-life regression can also be done through self-hypnosis. It works, though generally not as well as if you journey with the aid of a professional.

EXERCISE
· ·
Rediscover Your Lost Gifts

For this exercise it's a good idea to do a voice recording of the regression so you may play it as a guided meditation. Or, if possible, have someone else read the regression exercise to you. As always, go somewhere you can be comfortable. Bring your journal with you and allow enough time to visit your entire life and retrieve details. You don't want to be interrupted.

Take a few deep breaths and relax. Let that relaxation travel down from the top of your head to the tips of your toes. Take another deep breath and imagine yourself at the top of a staircase looking down. We will count with every step down; you will become more and more relaxed, getting closer to a place and a time that has everything you do with who you are today.

Take another deep breath and take your first step down the stairs.

Ten… heading down now. Nine… more deeply relaxed. Eight… going further down now. Seven… more deeply relaxed. There's nowhere else you need to be. Six… further down now. Five… half way, more deeply relaxed. Four… down deeper, now. There's nothing else you need to do. Three… almost there. Two… deeper down, and one… at the bottom now. Totally relaxed.

In front of you is the entrance to the most beautiful place you've ever been, the most amazing place you've ever seen. The colors are crisper and brighter, and the sounds add to your feeling of total relaxation. As you began walking through the space, you notice there is a bridge up ahead. In a moment you will walk over the bridge. When I count from three down to one, you will cross the bridge. Three… taking your first step on the bridge. Two… moving over, knowing that on the other side of the bridge is a time and place that has everything to do with who you are today. And, one… step off the bridge into a time and a place where you've used your psychic gifts before.

Is it light or dark out? Are you inside or outside? Are you alone or with others? Looking at your body, notice if you are a man or a woman. Then, by looking at your clothing and your surroundings, try to determine what year or decade or even century it may be. Look at where you are and gather as much information as you can. Who else is there? Where do you live? Do you work? What do you do?

Now, focus on your psychic gifts. How do you utilize them in this lifetime? Do you psychically hear? See? Feel? Know? Do you have the ability to intuit when someone needs healing and why? How are you using your gifts, and do you share them with others? Or have you denied them entirely or hidden them from everyone? Take a while to discover whatever else you can about your abilities in this time and place.

When you are ready, go back to the bridge. One … take your first step toward coming back to the present. Two … moving over the bridge, bring your psychic gifts with you. Three … step off, back to your current life, but with a greater metaphysical intelligence. Take a deep, clearing breath and open your eyes.

Grab your journal and immediately write down every detail you can recall. You don't want to lose it. Did you go to a previous life? Did you discover which gifts you had? Were you surprised?

. . . .

Give yourself a couple of days to uncover your newly matured abilities. Did this regression help to cultivate the gifts you already had? Did it ripen new gifts? Do you feel like it was easy to access your past lives and the psychic abilities you used during them? Sometimes it's just about giving yourself permission to experience your metaphysical senses. If you had an experience that caused you to be afraid of your gifts, you may discover you've closed them off. Past-life regression is one more tool in your tool belt to help advance your psychic abilities beyond a beginner level.

How Deceased Loved Ones Can Help

There is good news and bad news. Let's start with the bad news. You have probably lost at least one or more people that you care about. This is our reality. We are born, we pay taxes, and we love and have family, and then we die. Now, for the good news. Our loved ones are never really gone. They are on the other side, and they are rooting us on! They want us to succeed. And, they want to help us tap into our inherent gifts from our ageless spirit.

Just like us, their spirit lives on as well. They will always be linked to us, through our spirits, connected in a way that transcends time and space. We progress through our lives, learning and hopefully improving our souls, and our loved ones travel alongside us, both in the physical realm and the metaphysical. They aid us in our past-life discoveries and they welcome us to the other side and back again. And, they help us develop our gifts.

During a past-life regression, you can ask your loved ones to travel with you. We usually don't share the same relationship with each of our family members and friends throughout our lifetimes. Rather, we share the same group or pod. For example, in this lifetime we may be a man named John, married to a woman named Carrie with two kids, named Sarah and Jeffrey. In our previous lifetime, we may be Sarah, with Jeffrey as our mom and John and Carrie our best friends. We change our physical bodies, our genders, and our relationships, but travel with our familial pod.

We learn lessons throughout each lifetime and these loved ones are part of those lessons. We continue, generation to generation, trying to repattern what we've learned and brought into our lives. Breaking the cycle is crucial to moving forward. To illustrate, imagine your grandmother grew up impoverished and had a very difficult life, financially destitute. Then your mom grew up, stuck in the same scarcity mind-set, barely managing to stay afloat. Now, it's your turn. Have you learned the lesson yet? Or, are you going to go through life broke, expecting to stay broke?

Your peeps on the other side are there to break the psychic stigma as well. If you uncovered during your past-life regression that you hid your gifts out of fear of persecution, then it may be time to ask for help releasing your fears. If you weren't permitted to be your authentic psychic self because your grandparents or your parents didn't allow it, they are now ready to encourage and foster it from the other side. If you've forgotten how skilled you were, your familial pod will nurture and inspire you to recall your gifts. Essentially, they are your mates, the ones you will continue with until you are done learning from each other. They are the ones who know you best and can, along with your guides, help you raise your spirits. They want to be of service.

EXERCISE

Use Your Pod

In a quiet spot, close your eyes. Begin by breathing deeply, inhaling and exhaling with conscious intent. When you are comfortable, feel the energy in your toes. After you've detected the energy, move it up into your ankles and feel the warmth as it fills up your joints. Now, move that energy up into your calves and shins. Feel the heat move up into your knees and hips. Let your focus continue through your abdomen and your solar plexus. Up a bit more, now, into your chest and shoulders and arms. Continue this energy up through your neck and face. Move it all the way up, out of your crown chakra, allowing the energy to flow over your body.

Take another deep breath and imagine you are stand-ing in front of a tree. It is a beautiful tree with nice full branches. It has a thick trunk and it reaches up and out toward the beautiful blue sky. Streaks of sunlight shine down, surrounding you with the energy of the universe. Step closer to the tree. As you do, feel the energy of the earth connecting to your energy. Reach your arms out and hug the tree. Become one and let your mind, body, and spirit experience the connection.

Now, while still linked together, stretch your awareness out to the branches. This, you see, is your family tree. You have many family members and friends branching out, still attached to this life and on the other side. Spread your spirit through the limbs and extend outward, through the wood and the leaves until you feel yourself connecting to a de-ceased loved one, someone who was part of your family tree. It might be a family member or even a close friend. Ask for their name or initial so you can identify who they are. If you don't receive a name, state that only those with positive energy and intentions are allowed to be part of your tree.

Now comes the good stuff. Use your familial pod to en-hance your gifts. Ask this first person to heighten your psy-chic abilities. Ask them, "Do you have a specific psychic gift you want to help me with?" Wait for their answer. If they say yes, ask them to send the energy to you through the branches. Notice if you can tell which psychic sense they assist you with. If they say no, ask them to send whatever energy they can to augment your gifts. Be open to receiving the boost either way.

Continue making your way through all the branches in your family tree until you no longer feel you are connected to anyone. Then call your energy back. When you've pulled away, take a deep breath and release the tree. Thank your ancestors, friends, and family that shared their psychic gifts with you to help expand yours.

Open your eyes and breathe deeply. Check in with your body, mind, and spirit for any improvements. Do you notice any enrichments? Are you experiencing any kind of heightened awareness? Pay attention to anything that may feel different than before you connected to your tree.
. . . .

You might have noticed a strong connection when you worked with your family tree. You travel lifetimes together; you've built roots that meander through your current life and join with your familial pod. Learning from each other not only increases your general awareness, it enhances your metaphysical intelligence. It adds to your capability to progress from a beginning level or entry-level psychic student to a rank beyond. We usually pick up and absorb information every day. If we wait for it to come to us, we will glide along, probably happy, but never advancing past our current situation. But, if we decide we want more, it's up to us to extend ourselves to tap into it. Our family is there to help us achieve that.

You can look to your past lives as well as your familial pod to learn and make adjustments in this lifetime. Knowing that your cousin may have been your daughter in a previous life can also help explain why you may have an extra special connection to them. Appreciate that we don't have to start from square one with our psychic gifts—rather we can tap into the knowledge that we've gathered in our previous lives. We accumulate so much psychic wisdom; it would be silly to not reap the benefits by pulling it back up to our current reality. Knowing it's there adds an extra layer of security and can be harvested to take your psychic abilities beyond a beginning level, especially when practicing with other people.

CHAPTER 8

More Advanced Practice with Psychic Buddies

As with any friendship, it is beneficial to find some psychic companions. You may have already connected to others through natural friendships, online contact, development classes, common interests, or some other way. Having the opportunity to bounce ideas off each other, or to practice together, is beneficial when trying to deepen your abilities. You don't *need* someone, and you definitely don't need a full-time participant, but it brings a different type of challenge to your development. In addition, it allows you to work and receive feedback immediately, and from someone you can trust with at least some knowledge in the metaphysical realm. It makes it feel more alive and more real when you have an actual person to psychically play with—this keeps it fun and exciting!

Common Interests

Discovering people who enjoy the same activities as you brings you a greater level of fulfillment. Having friends who pursue other hobbies, apart from psychic ones, is also beneficial, as it introduces you to additional activities you may not have been exposed to yet. Hanging out with metaphysical practitioners is not necessary, but doing things with other like-minded people affords you more opportunities to bounce ideas and thoughts off each other because they understand what you're talking about. You might find that being able to share your psychic gifts with someone will attract you to them, and vice versa. If you are fascinated by the psychic realm, as I am, you may feel a longing to reach out to those who share the same ideas and desires.

When you begin exploring, you might feel as though you need to keep your pursuits to yourself, for fear of being exposed as someone who may be crazy. Let's be honest. Sometimes, especially in the beginning of your development, you may question your sanity. It can be scary if you have no one around you who shares your beliefs or ideas about what's happening. That's why it's so important to be around others with common interests to help raise your energy while you try to magnify and increase your abilities beyond the beginning level. Engaging with someone who understands or is experiencing something similar while advancing through this stage can be extremely beneficial.

Finding your tribe is not always an easy task. Just because you might both be interested in psychic abilities doesn't mean you are the same type of person, or more specifically, doesn't mean you have anything else in common. Personalities are also important. So, not only should you search for someone who shares the same metaphysical goals as you, you should look for someone you can connect to overall. A key concept to remember is that just like any friendship, your psychic friends don't have to check all the boxes for you. If they do, great. If not, it's totally all right; you can connect to each other metaphysically and leave the rest for other friendships.

Psychic Word of the Day

Exercising your psychic muscles will increase their capacity, just as working out at the gym does for your physical body. An easy way to do this is to find someone or a few people you can share a word of the day with, like one of your psychic buddies. My sister and I will tune in, briefly, to each other's energy at random times of the day and send each other what we call a word of the day. We ask to intuitively receive a word for the other person that can help or guide them. It often brings insight to things we need to work on, or it can direct us to what we should be on the lookout for or what's meaningful on that particular day. It doesn't matter if the other person is psychic or not; it can work with anyone who is open to allowing themselves to see, hear, feel, or think of a word.

There are two very different ways to share a word of the day. When you offer someone a word of the day, you can just drop it there and leave it alone, meaning you can just share with them whatever word pops into your mind first and give it to them with no explanation. It's their word and you can let them discover what it means, no matter what the word is, or even what their reaction is to it. Or, you can give someone your word for them and ask if it immediately resonates with them. Then, you can explain what it may mean for them.

For example, I shared a word of the day with my sister yesterday. I told her "red robe." She instantly knew it was something literal for her. She was editing her novel, which she was preparing to send to her editor, and she was reading a part where the main character was wearing red robes. We could have ended it there, as it made perfect sense and validated that she was doing the right thing and I was connecting to her. But, there was more. I told her the red robe also meant she needed to be confident with what she was doing. The red was about her foundation, her security. By wrapping herself in it, she would protect herself and could feel secure that she was moving in the right direction.

A word of the day can lead to an entire reading. By giving yourself a reading prompt, you are opening to the universe to begin receiving information about the person you are delivering the message to. It's like a writing prompt where you have a word and then write a story around it. Essentially, you can start with a word that you psychically receive and allow the story of that psychic connection begin to flow.

EXERCISE
· ·
Word Up

Grab a partner and decide who is going to begin. The sender of the word can breathe deeply and tune in to the receiver. Now, take another deep breath and on the exhale tell the person the first word you perceive. Don't judge it, don't question it, just say it out loud. Let them sit with it for a moment.

Now, let them tell you if it resonates with them in some way. If it does, great! If not, that's okay, too. After you've discussed it, dive into your intuition and begin deciphering the story of what the word is about for them. Explain what it may symbolically mean, as well as what it may literally mean to them. Give them at least a full paragraph of detail and continue interpreting it if you can. Then ask again if it resonates with them.

Did this exercise come easy to you? Did the initial word come easy but the translation was difficult? Or was the story easier than the word?

Try switching. Have your friend intuit a word for you. Does it resonate with you? Do you understand it? How about when they tell the story of the word to you? Does that make sense?

Find someone you can share a word of the day with on a regular basis. You might find it gets easier as you go, or that the words flow more naturally.

. . . .

Enjoy this process. You can take it to a deeper level if you desire by giving a full, in-depth reading as to what the word means, or you can keep to the fundamental basics by just presenting your partner with a psychic word. Change it up and give others the opportunity to experience the word of the day. Share your impressions with each of them in a different way and see how each delivery feels. You might discover presenting your messages in a variety of techniques can help you increase your own abilities.

Get into Heightened Practice through Circles

Having a safe place to practice with other like-minded individuals can elevate your spirit. I have always found being in a classroom, whether as the teacher or the student, helps raise the energy of the entire room. This means it increases your spiritual connections and your psychic gifts. Imagine the energy of a class full of middle schoolers who are all laughing—it's contagious. That's what it feels like when you share energy in a psychic circle. It enables everyone there to spiritually share and can increase the number of psychic hits for all who are reading.

It is crucial to find a circle where you feel comfortable. For instance, if you walk in and feel like everyone is trying to *take* your energy, you may not want to stay. This happens. Not always because they are trying to be intuitive thieves, but often because they need more from you than you need from them. But, if you get warm and fuzzy when you enter, there is a high probability they want to share their knowledge, wisdom, and gifts with you, rather than just funneling yours to themselves. That's where you want to be.

Finding the perfect circle can be an ongoing struggle or you might get lucky and discover one where you fit in. If you find you are stuck and have a hard time finding a circle that aligns with your desires and metaphysical goals, you can start one yourself. It's a good idea to join or start a circle with people who are on your level, but you may also want to invite and include people who are already a bit more psychically educated. It helps to have someone who can answer questions you may have. You don't want to be the most experienced psychic because you will find your development a bit stalled.

When you sit in circle, you create a sacred space where all are protected, and the fundamental goal is to connect to the universal energy for each other and yourself. One way to run the circle is to open with a meditation to raise the energy. Then you can have everyone tune in, focus on an individual in the group, or open to spirit and connect with whoever wants to come in. Then share the messages. Have each person take turns building on what the first person tuned in to. Another method is to have one person in the group act as the psychic, with all the others raising the energy by meditating and calling in the strength to boost the psychic's impressions. Rotate around the circle, allowing everyone the opportunity to share what they receive.

Remember, the purpose of a circle is to increase your gifts. Practicing, without pushing yourself, will not take you beyond a beginner level. Rather, it will leave you working exactly at the same level you've been. That said, utilize the energy of the circle. Allow it to raise your frequency to connect and provide greater evidence that you are truly connecting to someone in the circle or to someone from the other side. Think of this as a kind of psychic college training where you can study and work harder than you did in high school, but where you have more freedom to discover what you enjoy and which areas or abilities you thrive in. Being in a circle automatically produces a higher success rate for your connections simply by using the combined energy of the group.

Work with a Mentor

I am always asked if I mentor budding intuitives or professional psychics. The answer, unequivocally, is always YES! I believe having a mentor is extremely important. It allows you to share your hopes, fears, dilemmas, and celebrations with someone who gets it. It also gives you one-on-one practice and advice. Imagine having a teacher who can cater to you and your individual needs, someone who can address your questions and who understands what you're trying to accomplish. This type of psychic adviser can really propel you to the next level in your development.

Mentoring does not mean it is strictly a teacher-student relationship. A good mentor encourages someone else's growth, allowing them to find their own path. Having mentors at various points in your expansion can address specific areas you want to work on that will further your abilities. It's not just about enriching core psychic knowledge, it's the element of feeling comfortable using your gifts. Being able to trust in your mentor's abilities, as well as trusting them to shelter you, and hold the space for you to be your authentic self is a critical aspect of a mutually beneficial relationship.

Sue came in for a session during a girls' weekend event. While she waited outside the reading room, she recorded in her journal all her wishes and dreams, hopes and fears. She came in and we began the session, opening with my explanation of how I tune in to the universe and her guides before writing down everything I receive. I had a page full of notes ready for Sue, messages and intuitive impressions that I began sharing. Her jaw, as the session progressed, dropped further and further toward the floor. The reading addressed everything she had been writing about. While she was somewhat shocked and overwhelmed that our notes paralleled each other's, she was fascinated that her guides had shared with me what she needed to hear. There was also an element of telepathy, where I was tuned in to her thoughts and what she wrote. Although my meeting with Sue was not a mentoring session, it is a great example of how a mentor and student can practice connecting and working together.

Many practicing psychics offer mentoring services. Many life coaches do as well. It is not critical to have a professional psychic or medium mentor you, as a coach can also encourage you and bring out a lot of your natural talents. Though having a psychic help train you can be beneficial, as they will understand how to connect in certain ways, it is not crucial—coaches will foster your gifts in different ways. Someone who can be there to answer questions is the best type of mentor. A coach can be a great first step if you are not able to find a psychic who is up to the task. Remember, all developing psychics are at different levels and need different types of help, so it's not a one-size-fits-all thing. Be open to different types of mentors to get the best type of assistance for yourself.

EXERCISE
. . . .
Writing Together

If you have a mentor, use them for this exercise. If you don't, grab a fellow extrasensory friend and sit in two different rooms, or at opposite sides of a room, with your backs to each other. You will play both roles, but you will do the reading first. For this to work, you must be honest about your hopes and dreams, and even the fears you have. Your intention for this exercise is to see whether you're able to connect to a mentor (whether it is a true mentor or your friend acting as a mentor) using all your psychic gifts, as I did with Sue.

You, the "student," will give the other person five minutes to begin. The "mentor" will be honest and write down everything they want to know about, beginning with their aspirations all the way to their worries and doubts. What-ever they write about, such as current situations, people, and so on, must be real; they need to be true to allow the student to do their job.

After five minutes, you will tune in to the energy of the mentor, picking up everything the universe has to tell about the mentor and the mentor's loved ones. You will write down everything you receive. Then the mentor will join you and start sharing what you wrote.

The idea is to give everything you got, don't judge or question. Let the mentor respond to what you told them, but with a twist. Compare what you wrote down and see if you've addressed any of the things the mentor wrote down.

Have the mentor go down the list they made, item by item, and ask yourselves if the reading translated anything or any answers that related to what the mentor asked. If not, did the reading resonate with the mentor in different ways? It's important to try to connect to the information the mentor deemed important enough to write down in this exercise.

When you are all done comparing, switch roles and see if it works better for you. Again, the goal of this exercise is to try to connect to someone on a different level.

. . . .

A good mentor relationship will provide you with guidance and direction. They can't give you psychic abilities; their goal should be to help you excavate and recognize the gifts you already have and teach you how to develop them further. They can also assist you with the progression of moving from beginner to beyond beginner.

Surrounding yourself with psychic buddies, regardless of whether you are in a student-teacher relationship or you are on equal footing, will raise your frequency and theirs. You can exercise your psychic abilities with other people as often as you want. You will see that becoming friendly with other developing psychics can provide you with a lot of fun while you practice. I believe hands-on learning is the best. Staying connected with people you can train with gives you that opportunity. If you still find it difficult to find others like you, look on the internet. You might find groups that offer circles or meetings. There are also a lot of spiritualist churches that are, for the most part, non-denominational. Also look on social media for keywords like *psychic* or *psychic development* and you will find a multitude of practitioners as well as budding intuitives. Who knows, you may end up meeting your best friend this way!

CHAPTER 9

···

From Intermediate
to Professional

It's a good indicator you may want to start reading more when you're comfortable with your abilities and feel like you're ready to help other people. You will likely feel drawn to reading for others on a regular basis. It is important, however, to get their permission before tuning in to them psychically as you don't want to be intrusive. You will probably find the more you're able to read for others, the more people will reach out to you to help them in some way, usually through word of mouth. This is a great step toward becoming a professional.

At this point in your development you may feel the urge to begin offering some type of professional services. You can start off slowly or go full speed ahead; it's your choice as long as you're ready. Becoming a professional isn't just about your psychic abilities, though. There is more to it than merely using the skills you've developed. Learning how to be ethical and how to proceed is almost as important as your metaphysical intelligence.

You Don't Have to Have It All to Move Forward

The key to moving forward with your practice is knowing you don't *have* to know everything or be able to do it all to progress. Each gift or level of development comes with a sense of pride and ownership, which feels wonderful. But, attaining new skills is not the only thing you should focus on. Learning more within each ability is just as crucial to expand your abilities. Bringing your talents along through every aspect of your development will serve you well with your overall growth. Think of your development like a pond. With everything you learn or dive into, a ripple is created that extends throughout the entire body of water. This ripple contributes to and creates change throughout the whole pond, or your overall psychic awareness. This, in turn, allows you to continually increase your knowledge in the metaphysical realm. Lateral movement, discovering similar things while discovering the propensity for other gifts, is also forward progression.

Now is a great time to look back on everything you've done so far. Taking stock of your psychic inventory will help you better gauge what you've got a knack for and what you want to work on. Notice I didn't say "what you need." This isn't about needing to do anything. For you to move forward, you just have to want it. It is this desire that will keep you going—that and the effort you put into it.

EXERCISE
· ·
What You Know and What
You Want to Know

This is an exercise to review which psychic gifts you feel comfortable with and which you still want to work on. It's also a chance to evaluate which gifts you feel you want to develop further, because you feel you resonate with them. Get your journal and create a table like the one below, or fill this one in. Come back to the table as you continue practicing your abilities throughout the rest of the book.

Psychic Ability, Activity, or Tool	Comfortable	Need to Develop	Want More of This Gift	Set a Goal	Practiced with Others	Using Gift to Read Others
Clairvoyance						
Clairaudience						
Clairsentience						
Claircognizance						
Clairalience						
Clairgustance						
Psychic symbols						
Energy work						
Chakra system						

Psychic Ability, Activity, or Tool	Comfortable	Need to Develop	Want More of This Gift	Set a Goal	Practiced with Others	Using Gift to Read Others
Meditation						
Astral travel						
Psychometry						
Transfiguration						
Intuitive evidence						
Insight from past life						

Were you surprised at what you wrote down or what you feel comfortable with? Were you able to set goals for each item? Determining where you are gives you the opportunity to make a conscious effort to bring your gifts to the next level by working on your weaknesses and enhancing your strengths. Acknowledging you may excel at one gift or one tool can provide you with the confidence you need to move forward—remember, you don't have to have it all to go beyond, but you do need to be honest and ethical.

Ethics and Responsibilities

Ethics weave their way through every aspect of professionalism. This is especially true when you provide psychic readings. When people come to you, they trust you to have their best interests at heart when you provide them with a session. You direct them on what may be the most important life-changing events they will ever have. You may also connect them to their deceased loved ones and you want to be sure you know who you are working with. They are looking to you for guidance and you must give it to them without inserting your own opinions or ideas about their situations, regardless of how you may personally feel. You owe them a judgment-free reading. This is what they pay you for. You also owe them the truth, which you should provide them in a safe way, free of censoring, but given in love. Overall, you are responsible for their reading, and they are responsible for what they do with the information. This starts with a positive, ethically clean session.

When I first started I didn't want to just hang a shingle that said "Psychic" without being sure I knew what I was doing, so I set out to learn everything I could about psychic abilities. I wanted to be able to answer my clients' and my own questions about how psychic abilities worked. I studied with others and on my own to find out how others performed and connected. It is important to learn from the perspective of other practitioners as well—it supplies you with a deeper understanding of the way intuitives work. You need to be the best psychic you can be, otherwise you are doing your sitters a disservice.

Being ethical is crucial. You must be completely honest and truthful in your readings. You can't lie about the messages you receive, and you can't pick and choose what to tell your clients. What you *can* do is soften any harsh communications you get. You don't ever want to talk in absolutes. We have free will and can change the course of our lives depending on the choices we make. Share the best possible outcomes, rather than the worst, and how your sitter may arrive there. Don't deal in fatalities. If you are a medium, you never want to scare people with doom and gloom predictions, even if the client begs for it. You should, however, empower them. For example, if you see an accident, you could discuss new directions they may want to take to avoid an accident. Or share things with them they might want to avoid doing, which may cause the bad possible outcome you see. While it is your ethical responsibility to share what you receive, it is up to you to decide how to do that.

Essentially, you want to empower your clients by being optimistic. Regardless of what messages you receive, it's the delivery that you're responsible for. Sharing the information in a positive, life-affirming way will always trump any negativity or negative approaches. The purpose of giving a reading is to inspire someone to enjoy, improve, and make powerful their life. It is also to help them discover their greatness. If you connect them to their deceased loved ones through mediumship, it is even more reason to spread love and encouragement instead of negativity.

So, how do you turn something bad into something good? If you psychically hear your client is going to get fired next month, would you say, "You're going to get canned next month!" or "Now would be the perfect time to research other career or job possibilities. I think you might want to think about what you would love doing and begin interviewing for new positions now—it's the perfect time for you to start something new! It's a good time to let go of your old job!"? If they ask if that means they are going to lose their job, you can be honest, but again, in a productive way. "I do see that as a serious possibility, but I also feel you can find something better for yourself!" Again, it's about your delivery and the way you present the information to your clients. Do it with love, respect, and consideration and you will always provide a positive reading, regardless of what is coming through. You don't want to lie to them, but you can provide them with a different perspective. Sometimes, there's no good way to twist it. I always tell my clients to take what I say with a grain of salt. It's one possible outcome. They have freedom of choice, which can always change things and, besides that, we psychics are not always 100 percent right! We need to give them the information we receive and let them decide what to do with it.

Another way to be sure you always remain ethical is to devise a standard for yourself. I treat my clients as though they are my patients and I am their doctor. In other words, I use doctor-patient privilege, or confidentiality. I only share content from readings in books or with others when I ask for permission. Otherwise, their readings stay their own. I don't share client names or how they reacted to messages unless they give permission. This is their time and they need to feel they are in a safe place during one of their most vulnerable times. Many clients are so emotional they begin to cry while I explain my process of how I work. They are so worked up, sensitive and nervous, hoping to receive good news or to communicate with their loved ones, that they are already tearful. The air is also charged with the energy of the universe, specifically for them, so it can be an incredibly powerful time. This is no one else's business. Be responsible and compassionate—you hold their heart in your hand; don't crush it.

Don't Let Conflicting Sensations and Emotions Hold You Back

My husband tends to get very excited about things. He is a car buff; I'd like to refer to it as a hobby, but a hobby shouldn't cost this much! He recently finished restoring and souping up a 1967 Mustang. He has done a fine job and the car is amazing. Now comes the time to register it so he can drive it to car shows. He is so excited, he can't wait to get it on the road. *At the same time, he wants to throw up.* He is worried about going to the Department of Motor Vehicles. He is concerned they will ask him for more information, or that they won't register it. He has no real basis for this worry, he just feels it intensely because it's very important to him. He is also worried that if he drives it on the road, it will break down, and then what would he do? Here's the problem. He is mixing his extreme excitement with his fear, and it's overwhelming. He needs to separate the two, allow that there are always possibilities that something can go wrong, but that he is justified in being over-the-top happy.

Once he separated the two emotions, he went to the Department of Motor Vehicles and he registered his car with no problems. He had elevated his emotions so much he was in a whirlwind. Recognizing the two highly charged, distinct feelings weren't mutually dependent, he accomplished what he set out to do. Providing psychic readings can cause this same extreme feeling. Mixing the excitement of connecting with your gifts and the fear of being wrong or not receiving anything can keep you from moving forward and offering sessions. Holding each in its own space will expedite your ability to read for others.

When you have extreme passion, you feel things strongly. It's hard to stifle those feelings. This is fine if it doesn't hinder you or harm anyone. The problem that arises when you work with psychic abilities is that you deal with sensations. You count on your impressions to provide you with the information you need to share with your clients. When you have other feelings (that have nothing to do with the reading) clouding your perception, it can make it almost impossible to tune in and deliver a good session. Learning to separate the two can be crucial to move your psychic abilities beyond a beginner level. You will always be an emotional being, so separating your feelings from your psychic feelings will be a constant, ongoing process, but understanding the need to do that and learning how to discern the difference is essential.

EXERCISE

Separating and Understanding Your Overlapping Sensations

Discovering how to separate the sensations you experience starts with feeling the sensations and becoming comfortable with how they affect you. Allow your imagination to contribute to this exercise.

Close your eyes. Pay attention to how your body feels. Start with your heart and work your way out. If you are relaxed, you might feel a warm sensation spread through you. Notice how it feels as your attention moves out to your limbs and up through your neck. Now focus on how your head and face feel.

Next, imagine something in your life you are afraid of. Let it be something other than your psychic gifts. For example, if you are afraid of heights, imagine you are on the edge of a twenty-story building. If you're afraid of spiders, you might imagine someone dumping an entire bucket of them all over your body. Or, imagine a practical fear of not having enough money to pay your bills.

Now, focus on how your heart area feels. You might experience a more rapid heart rate or rapid breathing. Pay attention to how your body feels as you move your focus further out through your legs and arms, up into your neck. Are you feeling tingly? Is there a jumpy or nervous sensation creeping through you? Experience that feeling for a moment or two.

Then, take a deep breath and clear that energy. Think of something that makes you feel neutral, like a tomato or a tablecloth or even a random T-shirt. Focus on that for a moment, bringing you back to center. Try to empty your mind. Don't worry if there is anything trying to hold on; acknowledge your thoughts and then release them.

Finally, imagine getting ready to do a reading for someone. Think about how you connect, whether it's clairvoyance, clairaudience, claircognizance, clairsentience, or some combination of them. Now, focus on how it feels in your body. Again, start in your heart area. Do you feel little palpitations of excitement? Or trepidations as your nerves spark? Notice how your body feels as you imagine tuning in. Feel the sensations in your arms, legs, head, and solar plexus as you think about connecting to your guides and those of someone else.

When you are all set, process how it went. What did you feel? Did each situation feel totally different? Did it feel the same? Did you notice how the sensations may overlap? You can continue practicing this with other thoughts, situations, and emotions at any time. Figure out how each condition affects you and whether it's similar to your psychic sensations.

Discovering how each situation affects you can contribute to how you comprehend your psychic gifts. Knowing how it feels in your body when you experience any type of ESP or extrasensory perception will help you develop your abilities even further. Clear the sensation that's not pertinent to the situation. Understanding how to separate the extraneous sensations from the intuitive ones gives you a leg up toward taking your gifts beyond a beginner level.

Celebrate Failure

We are taught from an early age to celebrate winning. If we play a sport, the whole point is to beat your opponent. If we apply to college, we celebrate the acceptance letter. If we search for a significant other, we celebrate finding a match. We rarely celebrate the failures, or we forget about them in lieu of celebrating our wins. How about looking at it from a different perspective? Losing a game may help teach us to cope with disappointment. Being denied admission to our college of choice may provide us with an alternative school that accelerates our degree, and we might meet lifelong friends there. Being snubbed or dumped leads you to being introduced to your incredible future partner. Celebrating failures while developing your psychic abilities is very similar. Not being able to connect to someone's energy using your clairvoyance, or not "seeing" anything for someone, may enable you to change your method and instead use your clairaudience to "listen" for information. Doing this simple switch can grant you access to even more evidence than you could have hoped for to help yourself or your client.

I did a reading for Christine recently. Before she came in for the reading, I tuned in to her energy. Normally the information I write down first are character traits or physical appearances. This time was different. Instead of writing down basic descriptors about my client, I wrote two simple words for Christine: "I CAN." Next to that I wrote, "This is your new mantra—say aloud every day, at least three times a day!" At the time, I had no idea why I had written it, or why. When I told her that was the first and most important part of her reading, it was prolific. I had no idea it would cause such an outpouring of emotion and tears. Apparently, she had been going through a rough patch, as she often seemed to with her work. As she described it, everything she was doing for work was just good enough, but she never felt like it was great. She was at yet another crossroads with the programs she offered and whether she could continue, and more than that, if she could make it great. She felt like everything she did failed, and failed miserably.

I received a message from Christine today. Her daily disposition, as well as her life outlook, seems to have changed from a place of failure to a place of "I CAN."

"You told me my mantra for the year was 'I CAN,' and it has been in my head this week. It's helping me with everything I have to deal with. So many commitments that I would normally say, 'No, I can't do that!' to, I am saying 'I CAN' and things are moving right along."

She learned from her failures. She took advantage of the wisdom she had gained, and instead of continuing to view her previous efforts as failures, she looked to them as learning blocks. Obviously, she was now on her way toward celebrating not just her previous fails, but her soon-to-come victories. Everything in life is dichotomous. There are two sides and we need to keep the balance—good and bad, just and unjust, fair and unfair, black and white, yin and yang, boy and girl, dog and cat, fast and slow, power and weakness, struggle and ease. Celebrating failure allows you to own both contradicting sides from one situation.

EXERCISE
. . . .
Celebrate Your Failures

Grab your journal and open to a fresh page. Draw a line down the middle. On the top of the left side write "Failure" and on top of the right side write "Celebrate." Now, think back to a time when you felt you failed at something. It could be a relationship or a work issue or a personal attempt at something. Write that down under the "Failure" column.

After you've written it, stop and think about what you wrote. Then, think about what good came out of it. What positive turn of events came from that particular failure? Record your answer in the right-hand column under "Celebrate." If you're not sure, leave space for now. The positive results may not have occurred yet, or you might remember them later. Continue writing down more failures, leaving enough room to record a lot of celebrations next to them.

Now, record any failed attempt at psychic readings. Possibly during some of the previous exercises you've had a hard time connecting. Write these down. Maybe your celebration was simply the desire to continue learning, or that you were able to perform the tasks in a different way, one you never knew you could do. Also think of any times you tried to use your pre-cognitive skills (intuiting the future) that didn't work out. Did anything come from that? Write down your celebrations.

. . . .

While many failed attempts at successfully using your psychic gifts may drive you to quit trying, you've come quite a long way to let any failures keep you from succeeding. Understanding what you can learn from your ineffective endeavors can provide more wisdom than success at times. Just remember, your efforts do not go unrewarded. You learn from everything you do, and your attempts to tune in are not in vain. Often, it is merely time that is necessary to progress, and every exercise you cannot perform is not in futility—it may just require repetition to prove fruitful.

Fighting Off Your Inner Skeptic

I am one of the biggest skeptics I know. I always try to debunk if someone feels haunted or if someone is having what they believe to be paranormal occurrences. I also look for more than just a generic reading and I have a hard time trusting a psychic I feel doesn't have their client's best interests as their agenda. I am also always challenging myself to try to fight off my own inner skeptic regarding others and myself. I, like many of you, want clear evidence. I need the wow factor. I want immediate validation that what I share with my clients is, indeed, coming from the universal energy or the other side and not just my imagination. This always keeps me on high alert during a session. It creates a feeling of exhilaration before the session. It can also mess with psychic abilities. When you do professional readings, you must give what you get; you can never be skeptical. It holds you back and censors the information that may mean nothing to you, but can mean everything to your client.

You can't tailor a session to what you expect to get or what you think you should present to whomever you are reading for. You also can't censor the information you receive because you think it doesn't make sense. Your inner skeptic will always try to discourage you, even tell you, in a not so subtle way, that you're wrong. It can create confusion and even disorientation during your session and will often create a sense of doubt that will cloud every perception you have.

Pushing aside your inner skeptic can allow you to be more receptive to psychic messages. It keeps you from diminishing the possibilities that you are connected and helps you to translate successfully what you tune in to. Being a healthy skeptic, however, is all right. It means you don't jump to automatic conclusions for everything and you expect to feel some type of connection. This is okay. It's okay to not believe every situation, but also be open to what's coming, regardless of whether you immediately understand it or not.

I was at a women's retreat a few years ago. I met a friend named Jen there, and she was getting ready to leave. She looked at me and asked, "Okay, so I just want to know ... what do you get about me? Is there anyone who wants to tell me something?" Now, this is a very generic question, and normally it opens a stream of psychic visions, but this time I was just getting one thing.

"Why am I seeing a cow?" I laughed.

"Well, hmmm. Are you saying I'm going to get really big and fat?" Jen asked, shocked, but with a giggle.

"Ha!" I responded. "No, but I am definitely getting something about dairy. Like, do you love milk or cheese or something? Dairy allergy? What is up with the dairy?"

Now, if I had been skeptical, I would not have told her about the cow or taken it further. But, I trusted my intuition would give me information that could be interpreted.

"All right. Tell me about dairy. Obviously, there is something to this, but I'm not quite getting what it is. You have a big connection to it, though, in some way," I shared with her.

"The only thing I can think of is that I grew up in a town called Derry. It is not spelled the same way, but could that be it?" Jen asked, serious now.

"Ah, that absolutely is it. Your loved ones are letting you know they're around. They are sharing where you are from as evidence," I told her.

We then went on to discuss her experiences there, in Derry. Even though it was, essentially, a free reading, I still felt I needed to give her accurate information. If I had let my inner skeptic override my psychic impression, we would not have connected. Jen wouldn't have known her family members from Derry were reaching out to her, and I would not have known that I was really tuning in.

Free Readings

Once you've progressed past the beginning stage of psychic development, meaning you are more right than wrong with interpreted messages and you're comfortable with your abilities, you may be itching to qualify your gifts by offering regular readings. If you find yourself in an intermediate or even advanced level of intuitive development, you might want to start working your way toward becoming a professional. Working for free sounds like an oxymoron. However, doing free readings pays you in different ways. It allows you to practice in a professional environment, without the pressure of needing to provide a reading for someone's money. It does not mean you should treat the reading as anything other than professional though. You are still providing guidance to someone who is counting on your advice. Offering free readings in the beginning helps you grow your confidence as a consultant. You need to have faith that what you're doing for others is in their best possible interests and the information you bring through is clear from your own judgment and censorship. Providing free psychic consultations brings you a deeper awareness and gets you ready for your professional career.

When you offer free readings, it takes the pressure off you. The idea that you give a reading to someone when they are paying for it can cause you to cloud your reception of messages because you are so intent on making sure you are giving them their money's worth. Paying for something creates a higher expectation and that puts an added burden of stress on you to get everything right. By not asking for anything in return, you are free to focus on your work instead of the result.

Giving free readings does have a different dynamic in comparison to a paid reading, though. When you give away a reading, there is no exchange of value. When you don't charge for the session, some people don't associate a great deal of worth with it. If it doesn't cost them anything, they may not listen to what you have to say as much as they would if they paid for the session. So, it might behoove you to ask for some type of alternative energy exchange. Have them send you positive energy or pull a couple of oracle cards for you. They don't need to be psychic to offer you these small tokens of appreciation that can be good for you, and, more important, it will make them value the reading more.

Providing free readings can be kind of tricky. You can offer them to your friends, but you want to try to work with people you don't know as well. Reading for strangers allows you to deliver an unbiased and non-judgmental session, rather than one you inevitably interlace with your own thoughts and feelings. You can extend an offer for a free reading to your friends and followers on social media, explaining you are practicing and offer no guarantees. Another great way to find clients is to ask your group of friends to extend the invitation to their friends. Be sure to let everyone you give a reading to know to take what you say with a grain of salt. You are providing these readings to fine-tune your gifts and it's up to them to decide what to do with the information you provide.

Your Process

Your process can be an important part of offering readings, no matter the type. It offers you a structure where normally there may be none. I have established a process in my business and it's remained pretty much my standard for quite a while.

Before every reading, I tune in to my client's energy. I write down everything I receive from the universe about them. I include the basics about them, which helps me get into their energy, such as looks, personality, characteristics, and even hopes and fears. I will also write initials or names of any of their deceased loved ones who give me information or want to connect. I include any current, past, or even future events I receive, and I share dates or locations that I get psychically. When my clients come in, I begin the reading by going over everything I have on my paper—this usually opens us up to things they may want to know about or have questions about. Believe it or not, it usually fills the entire session time. I also tell clients I will not remember what I tell them, and I may not even recognize them or their name after the session. The information I receive is channeled through me, for them, and I don't hold on to any of it! In fact, I have to tell them to remind me of sessions if they want to be included in my books—this usually jogs my memory of the reading enough that I am able to write about it. Your process should be your own, just as my process works for me. Develop a procedure that works for *you* and helps you get into the energy of your client. You are on your way to become a professional.

No matter what your aspirations are, psychic or otherwise, you need to live by a code of ethics. This should be your standard, regardless of what you do, but very important with psychic work. We are also responsible for our thoughts and our actions. Our thoughts become our reality. We need to rethink how we think. Celebrate your failures as well as your successes. Believe in yourself, and be open to receive and give psychic messages, even if that means you must temporarily battle your inner skeptic. I say temporarily because once you begin the battle, your inner skeptic shrinks. A healthy amount will persist, but the cynicism will start to dissipate and what remains will be laced with excitement rather than fear.

CHAPTER 10

Going Professional: Sharing Your Gifts with the World

You've done so much work throughout this book. Before you picked it up, you probably wondered, "Now that I've gotten to this point, and I know about psychic abilities, what more can I do? What is out there for me? How can I continue to progress and how can I share my gifts with the world?" These questions are all valid and extremely important stepping-stones on your journey. They are the questions you should ask yourself. When I studied with my various teachers, I loved it. I knew, though, that there was always more to do, more to learn. Even now, I like the educational process. For me, part of that yearning to learn gets quenched by writing books and teaching, but I still thoroughly enjoy learning. We want to know, logically, what's next.

Now What?

Now that you've developed beyond a beginner, you may wonder what your next move should be. You need to think long and hard about what you want to do and tune in to your intuition to decide what feels right. There are many options available to you, including the choice to continue your education and practice more. Think of it like any type of therapy profession; you need continuing education units (CEUs) to maintain your license. Even though you don't need a license to practice psychically, you should always take advantage of learning opportunities to expand and introduce additional concepts to your metaphysical self. Remember, when you are in a learning environment, it raises the energy of everyone present. This, in itself, is worth it.

Chances are you are *not* done. You've discovered a talent within you that, once discovered, cannot be ignored. You are not done by any means; in fact, you are just beginning. A whole new world has been opened to you, to help your life have even more meaning than before. You've begun a process that is amazing, and can be terrifying, but you've taken that plunge. No, you are not done. But, what do you do?

Now is when the real challenge begins! What do you want to do with your gifts? Do you want to keep them to yourself and only tune in for you? Do you want to just read for family or friends? Or, do you want to become a professional and hang that psychic shingle? If so, there are several ways you can showcase your psychic prowess.

There is nothing that says you need to focus on becoming one type of psychic professional. Go with who you are and what your personality is. Some of us, myself included, get bored when only offering one service. I enjoy the variety of offering many different options to my clients. I have also discovered that I increase my abilities in other areas when I utilize my gifts in a diverse way.

Professional Psychic Reader

You don't need to pigeonhole yourself when it comes to your profession. You have options if you're ready to offer psychic assistance to people. Doing general psychic readings allows you to encompass a little bit of everything. You may be proficient at predicting the future psychically or by precognition. Or you may be good at tuning in to someone's current life. You might also be able to see into their past and how it affects their present as well as their future. And, if you're like me, you don't let any labels hold you back from including whatever comes through during a session. Offering general readings can give you a platform to everything psychic. For someone who is developing all their skills, this can be a good solution.

Setting up a practice to offer readings can be done relatively easily. Deciding where you want to set up shop is the first step. You must decide what works for you, personally. Consider whether you have to worry about finances while you start up your business. This may help you decide whether you want to begin doing your practice full time or part time. Do you want to advertise? Or do you want to stick to word of mouth? There are many places you can promote your business, starting with social media. Creating a separate profile page for your new psychic business on Facebook, Twitter, LinkedIn, Instagram, and other social content forums can be quick and easy and often free. Beyond that there are local and national print and online magazines, such as

Natural Awakenings Magazine and *Bellésprit Magazine*. These can be relatively inexpensive and are directed toward people who are interested in all things metaphysical and healthy. You can print business cards and flyers and distribute them around your community on bulletin boards in stores and metaphysical shops. Contacting local radio stations or online radio stations to interview you (if you're comfortable enough) to give the audience a sample of your skills will multiply your exposure. You can ask all your friends and family to share your information, along with a glowing review of your abilities. These are great ways to begin getting your name out there. Recognition is key and repetition breeds recognition, so the more you can saturate your market, the better off you'll be.

Now you need to decide where you want to give your readings. Do you want to hold sessions exclusively over the phone? If so, you don't need a physical location to offer your guidance to others. You need only have good cell service or a landline to do readings. Many people worry that it is more difficult to connect when you are not physically together. This is not true. Energy is energy and it travels to and from your client and yourself. Skype and FaceTime are also convenient options, and Skype has a free app and FaceTime comes with an iPhone plan. If providing readings in real time is a bit inconvenient or scary for you, you can start by offering readings over e-mail. Have your clients send you a couple of questions and then tune in and get the answers at your leisure. Phone and computer sessions are a great way to start with no or very little overhead.

If you are ready to do in-person readings, think about whether you want people coming into your home or if you want to go to their homes. If they come to your home, do you need a separate entrance? Will you feel comfortable allowing strangers into your private space or would this limit who you read for? Going to your client's home can work if you don't mind driving. However, there are a few things to consider. You might find the energy of someone's home disrupts your flow or creates confusion. Going to a local coffee shop is also a possibility but be prepared for noise and interference. These locations may present you with additional distractions; phones, pets, or even family can interrupt you and stall your connection. Having clients come to your home or you going to theirs can create an increased feeling of vulnerability, but it is also a very cost-efficient option.

Being with other like-minded individuals may help you feel comfortable and it might also increase your visibility. There are many healing or metaphysical centers that offer space for rent. There are also spiritual or metaphysical stores that hire readers for a few hours or a couple days a week—some have a set rate and others let you charge what you want and take a percentage. If you decide to go this route, you can work out of multiple locations. You might also find that you enjoy doing group sessions and having the space to do them at someone else's store can also help to promote the events.

Having your own office affords you flexibility and the opportunity to hold a variety of sessions whenever you want. It gives you independence, without having to clear your schedule or check the availability of someone else's office that you are sharing or borrowing. Having your own space allows you to create an office that you love. You can fill it with furniture, paintings, music, tapestries, crystals, and anything else that makes you comfortable. Being content and cozy in your own place can make it easier—you create the energy and can readily clear any unwanted energy to make it a more relaxed session. You have enough to be concerned with without having to acclimate yourself to a foreign space.

As with what type of psychic readings to offer, it is entirely up to you where you decide to host them. You can mix it up and do several things. Phone sessions along with metaphysical centers can give you a steadier flow of clientele. Working out of a store can score you some group readings hosted by your client at someone's home. Be open and willing to trust it will happen when and how it is supposed to. This is your life and you have made the choice to go beyond your beginning, so enjoy it, however it works for you.

Medium

Death is an inevitable part of life. The person who passes to the other side is busy learning and reviewing their lifetime on earth, but they are not in pain and are not sad. The friends and loved ones they left behind are the ones who suffer. They want a way to alleviate their pain and will often look to mediums to channel their loved ones. You can choose to be a professional medium and help others deal with the grief of losing their precious family member or friend. You will need to provide evidence that you are genuinely connecting, so be sure before you advertise yourself as a medium, you have developed your channeling to that level of expertise. With this gift, you can ease the pain of so many.

When you are a professional medium, you use your psychic gifts and it can overflow to include not just talking specifically to their deceased loved ones, but also what they have to say about your client's past, present, and future. Often, you just fall into mediumship. Connecting on a psychic level frequently leads to offering mediumship as well. If it's meant to be, it will be. Don't force it, but don't restrict it either. You want it to happen for the right reasons.

Right now, it seems to be the fad to become a medium. With all the mediums on television, it has become a household thing. However, offering this service should be done with integrity. You don't want to make anything up just to be a medium. You should not want to do this work for the money or fame. That is never a good reason and it will never pan out. Remember, karma is around to right wrongs, and acting like a medium when you're not connecting will always backfire. Don't offer mediumship under false pretenses. Do it because you love it, and you can't help but connect.

Having the ability to offer proof will help you determine whether you are ready to offer mediumship sessions or not. That proof does not have to be any one particular thing, just enough that the person you read for has what they need to recognize their loved ones. For example, Mary reminded me of a reading I did for her and her mom. I had tuned in to Mary's brother who had recently passed at a young age. I told them I was getting a *J* name.

"That was his name, Jerry," they replied in unison.

"No, I'm hearing another *J* name that was there to welcome Jerry with open arms when he got there," I continued.

"Hmmm. Well, my father was also Jerry. My brother was a Jr.," Mary explained.

"Okay, he's around you as well, but no. There is another *J* name that was there for him. I feel her death was self-inflicted,

which indicates it was her fault in some way, not necessarily suicide but caused by her actions," I relayed. I felt strongly that this
person was a recent death and I shared that with them as well.

"Oh my," her mom said. "That was his cousin, Jennifer. She
died six months ago, before him, of a drug overdose. No one
knew that. No one has even connected her to our family at all.
Nobody knew. How did you?"

They were both shocked, and it showed. They were perplexed
about how I was talking with Jennifer. I told them I could feel
their connection and that they were together, as they had been
before in life.

"Their children played together," Mary confirmed.

Being able to bear witness to the reunion on the other side
was the proof they needed to know I connected. Mary reminded
me of the reading because as usual, I didn't remember it. I don't
recall most readings I do. I just channel the information for my client. Not retaining the messages because they are merely passing
through you to your client can be one way to know if you really
connect or not, and if you are ready to offer this type of service.

Medical Intuitive

Being a medical intuitive usually means you need some biology
knowledge to read someone with any accuracy. Becoming familiar with the systems and functions of the body can help further
your career. Having said this, it's not a deal breaker if you don't.
You can just give as you get without trying to figure it out further. For example, I often receive information about blood or circulation. These, for me, are common references for either heart
issues, leukemia, or some other type of blood disease. For you, it

may mean something different. Learn to trust your body-scanning abilities. Most important, with this line of psychic readings, you want to not censor any information and double-check whatever information you receive with your guides before sharing it. Your clients and loved ones will depend on you and, more often than not, listen to your diagnosis. Remind them, as I do, to always take what you say with a grain of salt, that you're not a doctor, and they should consult one, if necessary.

I have read for people with all types of problems. From a common allergy to cancer, people will look to you for guidance. You cannot tell them something you don't know. You're better off telling them you're not able to connect to what they're asking about if you're unable to tune in to the specific thing they question. Don't try to alleviate their stress by telling them all will be good if that's not what you're getting. But always remember, your delivery is extremely important, especially with such a sensitive topic. If you are picking up on something that can be healed or needs a quick fix, you should share that with them. Especially if that's the only thing going on.

Dan came in for a reading a few years ago. Unbeknownst to me, he was essentially coming in for a second opinion. He was going in for knee surgery and wasn't sure it was required. When we were almost done with the session, he asked if there were any health concerns he needed to be aware of.

"I'm sensing something around your right knee. I feel like it's out of alignment or something. It almost feels like someone moved your leg over from the knee down," I told him.

"I was wondering if you would pick up on that. Do you think I need surgery for it?" he asked.

"I am not a doctor and I urge you to see one, but what I'm feeling is they could operate to put it back where it belongs ... like I said, it seems like it's moved over, but I don't feel like surgery is your only option. You might check on physical therapy, as I see an image of something sliding back on its own with work and support of a knee brace."

"Really? That's interesting," he answered with a perplexed look on his face.

"Listen, go to the doctor and get it checked out. I want to be sure you get fixed!"

"I did go to the doctor and they told me I needed surgery. I'm not convinced, which is why I came to see you," he shared.

"Oh. Well, why don't you talk to them about physical therapy and see if that's a viable option before you go under the knife?" I directed.

I didn't hear from Dan for a while. About a year went by before I ran into him again.

"Oh, hey! How's your knee doing?" I didn't know which path he'd opted for.

"It's great actually, almost like I never injured it!" he smiled.

"Awesome! So, did you have the surgery?"

"Nope. I did physical therapy for about two months. Like you suggested, everything slipped back into place. I couldn't be more pleased with the outcome," he answered.

It was up to Dan to determine which route to take. As a medical intuitive, you never want to diagnose or prescribe, but you can tell them what you tune in to and suggest they see a doctor. It is critical to remind them you are not a trained medical professional (unless you are) so they don't assume you know more than their physician.

You might feel yourself drawn to this line of work if you're already a medical professional. For some, this is an extension of their medical training, another tool in the med kit, so to speak. If you feel like this is something you want to specialize in and you have no previous medical training, it might be a good idea to take a biology or anatomy and physiology class to familiarize yourself with the body and its functions.

Pet Intuitive

To many, a pet can be a significant member of the family, not just an animal. Losing a pet can be just as devastating as losing a person. Communicating with them on the other side will help their human on this side deal with grief. You can also focus on pets who are still living. Animals do not speak a human language, so we need a way to talk to them and find out what they're going through or what they want. Being a pet intuitive allows you to help their people to help them get what they need. It can also let the humans know if the pet is happy with something they're doing or someone who is interacting with them. Offering services as a pet intuitive is perfect for someone who already feels a connection to animals.

I have always had animals as part of my family. I feel a deep connection with them and they belong with us. However, I don't feel I am particularly connected to them on an intuitive level. I do have client's pets come through on occasion and I can usually tune in to their live pets when asked. Being a pet psychic has never been my calling. Luckily it is for so many others.

To be a true pet intuitive or psychic, you want to be sure you are indeed connecting to a live or deceased pet. It helps if your human clients can give you feedback. Pay attention to how your psychic senses respond when you try to tune in. It's very similar to how you tap into a person's energy field. Pets can communicate much in the same way, though it may take a while to understand what they tell you. As with any psychic ability, practice will help.

Business Consultant

If you are business oriented or want to work in a more corporate atmosphere, you might consider becoming a psychic business consultant. This type of psychic can offer guidance to business entrepreneurs about new product viability or markets. As a business consultant, you will let your client know which direction they should take their business endeavors to better their company. You can also offer career guidance to anyone and everyone based on what you psychically pick up for them, like which career they are best suited for to reach their highest potential of happiness and success. If you have experience in the corporate world and continue to feel drawn to it, becoming a psychic business consultant may be a great career path for you.

Many people, including myself, leave the corporate world to begin a psychic career. Usually, this means you have some knowledge on how business works, or at the very least, have a grasp on what it means to work with other corporate employees. This can give you a leg up and get you started in this work. Qualifying your work with a signed disclaimer stating they are consulting with you and there are no guarantees that any business advice you give will further their company is a must—you don't want to provide warranties on anything other than the effort and time you put in.

When working as a business consultant, you do your best to tune in to whatever situation they give you and present them with the best possible options. Be sure you advise them on what you intuit regarding the options and how you feel they will play out. For example, if they ask whether they should open another branch in Florida or one in Maine, you can tune in to the locations using the weather. Do you feel warm? Do you feel cold? Do you see snow or sunshine? For me, I get the image of oranges when I think of Florida, and crisp, cold water over rocks and stones for Maine. The ability to use your psychic gifts in this way can help companies move or expand.

You may also be asked to go over employee files to see who to promote or hire or who to let go of or pass over. It may be difficult to be the one in control of someone's livelihood, so be prepared for this type of request. As a psychic business consultant, you may also help with investment opportunities, either deciding between a variety of presented selections or coming up with some choices on your own. The needs of corporations and businesses are essentially unlimited, as it will depend upon the type of business. But as a business consultant, it doesn't make a difference to you. Big or small, manufacturer, distributor, sales, or something else, you don't need to specialize—just using your psychic gifts will prove you're an asset to multiple companies and your ability will speak for itself.

Coach

Just like being the coach for a sports team, being a psychic coach or an intuitive coach allows you to help root your clients on. You can choose this path if you want to help others become successful in all aspects of their lives. Often called an intuitive life coach, you help your clients discover who they are and what they are most happy doing by using your intuition. You can also serve them well by helping them overcome barriers that may hold them back. By using your psychic gifts, you intuit what they need to work on to move forward. You can help them tap into their potential by tuning in to their intuition. You are there to applaud their successes and celebrate the lessons in their failures.

In my book *The Steady Way to Greatness* I discuss how we all have a greatness inside of us; we need only discover what it is and then figure out how to bring it to the surface. A psychic coach can help with this process. A coach can also teach clients how to manifest what they want to make them happier. Psychic coaches also guide their clients much as business consultants do. They help with relationship questions, and career and business endeavors by intuiting talents and desires and what their greatest potential is with each.

A good psychic coach will teach their client how to discover their talents. They should create a special synergy with their client so they can trust each other. A psychic coach inspires their clients and encourages them to be the best they can be by helping them tune in to their own intuitive gifts.

Mentoring

Your job as a mentor is to help others tune in to their psychic abilities. This may mean teaching them new techniques or helping them extend their psychic prowess to include new gifts. They may need help sharpening gifts they've already discovered. Mentoring is an ongoing process. You are there for your client on a scheduled basis or as needed, whatever you decide. Being a mentor also helps you practice your gifts because teaching allows you to learn with your students. If you like helping others, mentoring may be a great adjunct career while you offer readings or coaching. It is usually not a main psychic vocation, but rather a secondary, very beneficial one.

The main goal of psychic mentorship is to increase your client's overall metaphysical intelligence. Mentoring is not about being there 24/7 for your client. But, you do need to make yourself available to help them. Their gifts can flare-up out of nowhere, and they will need guidance from you as their psychic mentor. Setting boundaries is crucial, but you need to create a schedule that works for both of you. A mentor is someone who raises the psychic IQ of their client through practice, repetition, and exposure to new methods. A psychic mentor challenges their client to go further and deeper, perhaps stretching their gifts and abilities more than they expect. A mentor also answers questions that come up for their student. You are there to hold their hand and pull them to a new dimension.

Lecturer, Teacher, Presenter

Once you are at a point where you feel comfortable with your own abilities, you may find you have a natural desire to work with large groups of people. If you are already a teacher, it may be easy for you to transition into teaching others to use their psychic abilities. Lecturing and facilitating workshops can also be a good psychic career choice for you. You might even take it a step further and give psychic or medium demonstrations to audiences. If you feel relaxed teaching and speaking in front of others, you may have found your psychic niche.

Being a psychic presenter of any type often goes hand in hand with offering readings. Some people feel more comfortable going to a psychic in a group or watching them on stage. This is also a great way to reach a lot of people in a short amount of time. Being on stage can be daunting—it's all about your level of confidence. You must believe the universe will send you what you need to do a stage demonstration.

A while back I did a gallery event for more than a hundred people. I was very nervous. I never know what's going to come through. Turns out, I had nothing to worry about. My guides brought through a bunch of messages for the audience. I don't have a person my messages are directed to immediately. I narrow it down as I'm pulled in a specific direction. One of the things that comically stood out that night had to do with a toilet.

"I know this sounds strange, but I'm getting something about a bathroom; more specifically, a toilet," I said to the audience.

You think you know people, but you really don't until you mention bathroom. More than half of the people in the audience stood up and raised their hands, and the chatter started. "Oh, I've been having the hardest time going to the bathroom." "I'm so sick of sharing the bathroom with the whole household—we fight every morning!" "We really need to re-do the plumbing in our bathroom." "Ooh, that must be for me! I just changed the shower curtain this morning to a cute puppy one!" That's only a sampling of the audience response. You get the gist—there are a lot of things that happen in a person's bathroom.

I narrowed it down a bit. "I feel this message is for someone to my right, on this side of the room."

I pointed to the audience on one side and the people to the left lowered their hands and sat back down.

"Okay, so this is kind of funny, at least from my perspective," I chuckled. "The toilet broke so now there is a full-on renovation."

I looked to the audience and everyone slowly sat down, somewhat disappointed that it wasn't a message for them. I noticed two people whispering in the back of the group.

"Look, if you don't want to acknowledge this is for you, it's okay. But, they're not going away," I laughed.

The whispering couple stood up, giggling.

"My husband," the woman said, now full out laughing, "he went to use the bathroom and the bowl broke. There was water everywhere!"

"This apparently was the only way to get you to remodel the bathroom. She's been bugging you for years, now!" I said to the husband.

"So true! I should have listened to her," he said, looking lovingly at his wife.

Messages don't have to be huge and life altering. When you're doing group events, the participants will be happy with whatever comes through that connects them to their loved ones. Evidence can be brought, as simply as it was with the bathroom situation; it doesn't have to be anything more than that. Just proving their loved ones are around to see what's happening in their daily lives is enough; this is the good stuff, the comforting stuff.

Teaching large groups or lecturing is also a way to go. Using the energy of the students helps everyone raise their own frequency. It's like mentoring in that you help them discover their own gifts, but you also hold the space for them to practice with other like-minded people. I love watching their eyes light up as they discover just how incredible they are.

Author

If, like me, you've always been drawn to writing, becoming an author and sharing your knowledge and experiences in the metaphysical realm may be just what you've been looking for. It is easier than ever to share your wisdom through books with self-publishing. Or you can go through a traditional publishing house like Llewellyn. Remember, though, that there are a lot of authors who desperately try to get published, so it might behoove you to begin your writing career by building a platform of social media and e-mail followers. Beginning with a blog is a great way to start, along with submitting articles to wellness and mind, body, spirit magazines. If you feel like this is your true calling, don't give up. Trying to find an agent or a publisher can be extremely discouraging, but there is always a way to get published. Use your intuition to tune in and ask which way you should go. Tune in to get a visual of what your book or article looks like printed. This may give you an idea of who will publish it or how it will be published. That is exactly what I did when I submitted my query letter to Llewellyn.

I had already begun writing a "developing your intuition" book. I knew in my heart that I would be published. I wasn't sure how, but I felt it with all my being. I didn't want to self-publish; I knew I needed someone to help get my books out into the world. So, I decided to tune in to the spine of my book. I wanted to see what image or logo was printed there to show me who would publish me, a totally unknown, first-time author. What I saw shocked me. I was in a state of total disbelief. There was no way the moon I saw could be who I thought it was. But, I trusted my psychic abilities to lead me where I needed to be, and I looked up Llewellyn Worldwide online. Sure enough, they had a moon logo. I was floored. Llewellyn is a huge publishing house in this genre—there was no way.

I wrote a query letter to Llewellyn. My first ever. After a couple of days, I panicked, as most of us do when we don't fully trust. I began to research other publishing houses and sent out another quick query to someone, a much smaller company. They wrote back soon after with the typical "Sorry, but no." Then I heard back from Llewellyn. It was as if the clouds parted and my mom looked down on me from heaven and said, "Duh, I told you!"

I didn't know it then, but that first manuscript, *The Book of Psychic Symbols*, was just the beginning. Many books later, I am still going strong. You need to believe in yourself. If this is something you want to do, pick a topic (and there are many in the metaphysical genre) that you want to write about. Choose something you can make your own. Write about something you know or have personally experienced, not just something you've read about or researched. This makes it more personal and translates better to your readers.

Having the desire to write is the beginning. Following through and doing your due diligence will take you further on your path.

Being persistent is also crucial—don't give up! Write what you love and love what you write—otherwise it will show in your work. You will probably discover a few new methods to help you with your psychic work along the way as well. Enjoy the process.

Some Practical Tips

Knowing you are ready to bring your gifts to the world is not quite enough. You need to know how to go about doing this—after all, this is a business. Collecting payment, setting fees, establishing yourself publicly, and legal considerations are all things you need to consider.

Set fees based on what you feel you are worth. This is tough because we are all priceless. But, be honest with yourself. If you are just starting out, you do not want to charge exorbitant rates. Many psychics charge a dollar per minute to keep it easy: $30 for a half hour, $60 for an hour. You can start off with this rule of thumb and adjust and adapt as you see fit. No one can tell you what you should charge, but it is a good idea to check out what other local professionals charge, as well as others around the world. Remember, an exchange of energy is important to spiritually assign value to your reading, so money, as well as an equal barter, works well.

Collecting your fees is important. You want to set up a way to make it easy to get paid. There are per charge services that work very well. PayPal and Square are two you can utilize in person, over the phone, or through a computer, and for a small fee they simplify the process and make your client feel comfortable. Cash is always great in person, as well as a check, but be sure to get all their information before accepting a check.

Social media is a great way to get your name out there, as I said earlier. Advertising is, too. But word of mouth is one of the best ways to help share the availability of your gift with others. Having clients promote you based on their experience with you will bring clients from near and far. Ask your clients to write a review or share a positive post on their social media linking to yours.

Legally, you should always have your clients sign a disclaimer. Make sure you include that you are providing them a reading and they should use their free will to do what they want with that information. You are not a doctor or a licensed therapist (unless you are) and you do not prescribe or offer medical advice. Many areas require you to state that your readings are for entertainment purposes only. This is never a bad idea to include. Research what the legal requirements are in your area.

This is not a one-size-fits-all kind of job. With all the options available to you, including using your psychic abilities for only your personal benefit, there will be something you'll relate to. If you feel passionate about one type of career over the other, it may be easier to decide which you'd enjoy more. Being enthusiastic about many of the psychic career routes can also guide you in the direction you wish to pursue. Most psychic vocations overlap, leaving you with a multitude of choices. Choose something that challenges you enough so you don't get bored, but that you also feel comfortable enough with that you won't get discouraged. Above all else, do what you love and love what you do.

Conclusion

Undoubtedly, you possess an aptitude for all things metaphysical. If you didn't, you would not have picked up a beyond beginner's book. You have a calling and, dare I say, a duty to explore how far you want to take it. Communications between yourself and the other side have become easier and more expected. Your mind-set has changed, even as you read this book and completed the exercises, because as much as you already knew, you've gained even more wisdom. You've scrutinized your abilities and questioned whether you were learning much as you took your gifts deeper, but your psychic senses have become keener and more in tune.

You've gone back to the basics. Diving into the metaphysical realm is limitless, and you now have the wherewithal to continue swimming. Connecting to or reconnecting to your guides builds a stronger relationship and you've done that throughout the book. You are navigating your way through your extrasensory communications using your clair senses and it may feel strange or different or even exhilarating. All these emotions are great! It means you are stepping into your power, recognizing your multitude of psychic abilities. Having a bit of fear during your growth is quite normal; in fact, you should expect it. It's pushing through that fear and believing in yourself and your gifts that makes you go beyond a beginning level.

Just like with regular conversations, we use a language to psychically communicate. Extrasensory symbols are a normal psychic dialect. Our capacity to understand this form of nonverbal communication will continue to grow the more often we use it. And, our translations come faster and more detailed when we put in the time to practice tuning in. Use your symbols journal and be sure to leave plenty of space to consistently update it. This will ensure you can interpret messages that come in and will increase the span of symbols your guides and the universe will use. Basically, if you have a limited vocabulary, they will stick to that to help you comprehend what they send you. If you continually extend your scope and add to your recognized symbols, they will too. This is one of the best ways to increase your psychic abilities.

Channeling loved ones for yourself and others is one of the most amazing things you will do in this lifetime, and other lifetimes. Just imagine what you are doing. It's like a science-fiction movie, but so much better. Receiving messages and guidance from another plane of existence and being able to raise your frequency above the din enough to tune in is almost fantastical. It is mind-boggling that we work better in the extrasensory world *without* allowing our ego to sabotage us. Working *without* our ego will put us further ahead in the metaphysical realm.

You will find, if you haven't already, that the first time you experience any type of astral travel will just about knock your socks off. Seeing someone else's face superimposed or taking over your friends or clients is also astounding. You have the directions; you can revisit and practice both methods any time you want.

You are well on your way to becoming an even greater version of you! Don't stop now. You may continue your education and decide not to take it any further at this point. If you want to move forward and extend your personal gifts into a professional career, great! This is your time for learning who you are, intuitively, and what you want. Take advantage of all life has to offer. You may realize you are like me, always wanting more because you are so excited about all the metaphysical discoveries you are still open to.

Expect to feel different as you change. Your mind, body, spirit connection has been rejuvenated through the exercises you've done and all the reading your mind has taken in. The grass may look greener than before and the birds might sing a message to you. You may see through anyone that's trying to swindle or hurt you, and you might find a life partner right in front of you. All in all, you've made some incredible changes and with more time and effort, you'll continue to move forward with more confidence and increased self-esteem. After all, you deserve to be the best you *you* can be.

You are coming into your power in a very humbling way. Finding others who are working to do the same will not just help you practice, it will add to your fun. This should not be a chore; it should be an entertaining and exciting time. Remember, if you're repeatedly not enjoying it, maybe working with your psychic gifts is not for you. Or, perhaps you need to take a step back. Once you've given yourself a break, you can always come back. You can also pick and choose which gifts you like to work with and practice developing those more until you feel comfortable working with all of them.

Over the time you've spent reading this book, you've likely been thinking about whether you want to keep your gifts to yourself or share them with others. Offering free readings is a way to do both. Using your intuition and your psychic abilities for yourself, without the pressure of putting yourself out there and having to be right, may be for you. It offers you a great way to move toward becoming a more professional psychic, but allows you to take as much time and preparation as you need.

When you're ready, you may decide to do this work as your career. Becoming a professional psychic might be one of the best moves you'll ever make, but it can also be one of the most terrifying decisions. You will most certainly find yourself dealing with doubters and people who criticize you and proclaim you are irrational. (Believe me, it happens.) But, you'll know the truth. You are passionate about this because you are living in this psychic world. It's their choice if they want to play with you or not. Quietly standing up for the metaphysical system by continuing to provide evidential readings is all you need to do; that and support a platform for the next generation to build on.

I did a reading for Jaye. She e-mailed me with a several validations—blowing each of us away with the spot-on accuracy of the information I had channeled during her reading. She left happy, even overwhelmed, and bought a few of my books. The efficacy of the messages that came through was amazing; I am always happily astonished at how well spirit uses me. But, what really hit me, what truly made me value her e-mail, was what she said at the end.

"When we came home, I started reading your books to my young daughters. We did the third eye exercise, imagining a windshield wiper cleaning it off, while we were lying around Sunday morning. I read one of the meditations aloud and then we told each other what we saw. 'Blue, heavy round objects,' Maya tells me. 'I see a single bird,' Adeline tells me. It doesn't really matter what they are seeing, but that we are having this conversation: What is intuition? That was a beautiful conversation with them. We spent the rest of the morning enjoying another of your exercises, trying to move a feather with our minds."

That is fantastic. Believe in the extraordinary power that is out there to be tapped into. Enjoy every remarkable discovery along the way, as well as all your failed attempts. Celebrate the work you do with your soul and the energy of your guides and your familial pod. Step into your power and go beyond your own personal beginning. Appreciate your metaphysical intelligence—once it's yours, it can never be taken back!

Suggested Reading and
Words of Wisdom

Alvarez, Melissa. *Your Psychic Self: A Quick and Easy Guide to Discovering Your Intuitive Talents.* Woodbury, MN: Llewellyn Publications, 2013.

"Developing your intuition to higher levels is so beneficial. Think of it as standing in a doorway to the many different levels of higher consciousness and knowing that you can become one with all that is by choosing to grow the abilities that are part of your true spiritual being."

~Melissa Alvarez

Ambrose, Kala. *The Awakened Psychic: What You Need to Know to Develop Your Psychic Abilities.* Woodbury, MN: Llewellyn Publications, 2016.

"Awakening psychic abilities is timeless and universal and each person retains this intuitive information deep within their soul where they hold the key. When they are ready to remember who they are and why they are here, the inner door to the soul

opens and true wisdom (knowledge combined with experience) is revealed."

~Kala Ambrose

Chauran, Alexandra. *365 Ways to Develop Your Psychic Ability: Simple Tools to Increase Your Intuition and Clairvoyance.* Woodbury, MN: Llewellyn Publications, 2015.

"Developing your psychic abilities beyond a beginner level means treating your intuition like a discipline. It means practicing daily, perhaps rising early or staying up late; but most of all it means taking back your power from those who say it is wrong or silly and never squandering your power again."

~Alexandra Chauran

Choquette, Sonia. *The Psychic Pathway: A Workbook for Reawakening the Voice of Your Soul.* New York: Random House, 1995.

Dale, Cyndi. *Awaken Clairvoyant Energy.* Woodbury, MN: Llewellyn Publications, 2018.

"We're all inherently psychic, but how important to develop our gifts beyond that level. With a bit of work, we can fly instead of crawl, enjoy answers not only questions, see, hear, and feel the mysteries of the universe."

~Cyndi Dale

Dillard, Sherrie. *You Are Psychic: Develop Your Natural Intuition Through Your Psychic Type.* Woodbury, MN: Llewellyn Publications, 2018.

"When we begin to develop our intuition, it can feel like we are feeling around in the dark, not sure what we are searching for. Once we are beyond the beginning stage, the light has been turned on and everything is in technicolor."

~Sherrie Dillard

Holland, John. *Bridging Two Realms: Learn to Communicate with Your Loved Ones on the Other-Side.* Carlsbad, CA: Hay House, 2018.

Morning Star, Konstanza. *Medium: A Step-by-Step Guide to Communicating with the Spirit World.* Woodbury, MN: Llewellyn Publications, 2016.
"Advanced psychic development opens the door to spiritual teachings that expand you, giving you the tools for living a meaning-filled life."

~KONSTANZA MORNING STAR

Owens, Elizabeth. *Spirit Messages: Inspiring Stories About Mediumship and Experiences from the Other Side.* Woodbury, MN: Llewellyn Publications, 2018.
"We begin to realize how natural mediumship is as our abilities grow. Hopefully, that recognition will humble us."

~ELIZABETH OWENS

Rooney, Lisa Anne. *A Survival Guide for Those Who Have Psychic Abilities and Don't Know What to Do with Them.* Woodbury, MN: Llewellyn Publications, 2018.
"Just as important as what I gained by utilizing my abilities is what I lost, most importantly fear and anxiety. Being able to receive messages easier is a small part of truly connecting to your gifts."

~LISA ANNE ROONEY

Weiss, Brian. *Many Lives, Many Masters: The True Story of a Prominent Psychiatrist, His Young Patient, and the Past-Life Therapy That Changed Both Their Lives.* New York: Simon and Schuster, 1988.

Bibliography

Byrne, Rhonda. *The Power.* New York: Atria Books, 2010.

Judith, Anodea. *Wheels of Life: A User's Guide to the Chakra System.* 2nd ed. Woodbury, MN: Llewellyn Publications, 2006.

Kabat-Zinn, Jon. *Wherever You Go, There You Are: Mindfulness Meditation in Everyday Life.* New York: Hyperion, 1994.

Palm, Diana. *Mediumship Scrying & Transfiguration for Beginners: A Guide to Spirit Communication.* Woodbury, MN: Llewellyn Publications, 2017.

Pond, David. *Chakras Beyond Beginners: Awakening to the Power Within.* Woodbury, MN: Llewellyn Publications, 2016.

Smith, Gordon. *Intuitive Studies: A Complete Course in Mediumship.* London: Hay House UK, 2012.

Tolle, Eckhart. *A New Earth: Awakening to Your Life's Purpose.* New York: Plume, 2005.

Weiss, Brian. *Miracles Happen: The Transformational Healing Power of Past-Life Memories.* New York: Harper Collins Publishers, 2012.

Williamson, Marianne. *A Return to Love: Reflections on the Principles of A Course in Miracles.* New York: Harper Collins Publishers, 1992.

To Write to the Author

If you wish to contact the author or would like more information about this book, please write to the author in care of Llewellyn Worldwide Ltd. and we will forward your request. Both the author and the publisher appreciate hearing from you and learning of your enjoyment of this book and how it has helped you. Llewellyn Worldwide Ltd. cannot guarantee that every letter written to the author can be answered, but all will be forwarded. Please write to:

Melanie Barnum
℅ Llewellyn Worldwide
2143 Wooddale Drive
Woodbury, MN 55125-2989

Please enclose a self-addressed stamped envelope for reply, or $1.00 to cover costs. If outside the U.S.A., enclose an international postal reply coupon.

Many of Llewellyn's authors have websites with additional information and resources. For more information, please visit our website at
www.llewellyn.com

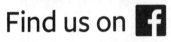

LLEWELLYN'S
Little Book of
PSYCHIC
DEVELOPMENT

MELANIE BARNUM

Llewellyn's Little Book of
Psychic Development
Melanie Barnum

Your psychic gifts are just waiting to be explored, and this pocket-size guide makes it easy! Discover how to tune in to your intuition, deepen your spirituality, and improve your relationships with simple techniques for developing your psychic senses.

Fill your life with abundance and positivity by engaging in your psychic birthright. This little book is packed with ways to help you, from hands-on exercises and journaling prompts to true stories from Melanie Barnum's clients and personal experiences. If you want to feel more connected to your spirit, make changes in your career, or receive help when making decisions in every area of your life, this is the right book for you!

978-0-7387-5186-3, 192 pp., 4.63 x 6.25   **$12.99**

MELANIE BARNUM

PSYCHIC
VISION

DEVELOPING YOUR CLAIRVOYANT
AND REMOTE VIEWING SKILLS

Psychic Vision
Developing Your Clairvoyant and Remote Viewing Skills
MELANIE BARNUM

Psychic Vision includes everything you need to know about using clairvoyance and coordinate remote viewing to enhance your life. Imagine being able to see people, places, or things without having to be there! With chapter-by-chapter exercises created specifically to take you on a clairvoyant journey, as well as complete instructions for utilizing the exact protocol used by the armed forces and intelligence agencies, *Psychic Vision* is an indispensable guide to developing your psychic sight.

978-0-7387-4623-4, 216 pp., 6 x 9   **$16.99**

To order, call 1-877-NEW-WRLD or visit llewellyn.com
Prices subject to change without notice

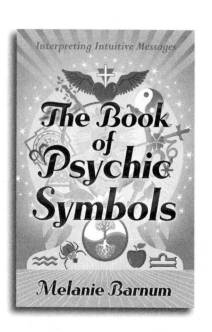

Interpreting Intuitive Messages

The Book
of
Psychic
Symbols

Melanie Barnum

The Book of Psychic Symbols
Interpreting Intuitive Messages
MELANIE BARNUM

A strong feeling, a remarkable coincidence, a strange dream . . . What may seem ordinary could actually be an important message: a helpful hint or a warning from a deceased love one or spirit guide. Open yourself to a wealth of guidance and opportunities by learning how to recognize and interpret the signs and synchronicities all around us. *The Book of Psychic Symbols* can help you decode dreams, intuitive flashes, and all psychic impressions. Intuitive counselor Melanie Barnum explains what psychic symbols are, how we receive them, and where they come from. She also shares amazing stories from her life that clarify how the wondrous intuitive process works. In addition to a comprehensive dictionary of 500 symbols, there are many practical exercises for exploring symbols in your life, fortifying your natural intuition, and using psychic symbols to manifest your desires.

978-0-7387-2303-7, 288 pp., 6 x 9 **$16.99**

Psychic Abilities for Beginners
Awaken Your Intuitive Senses
Melanie Barnum

There's more to this lifetime than the naked eye can see, and *Psychic Abilities for Beginners* is the perfect guide to this unseen knowledge. When you develop your psychic skills, you will increase your confidence, stimulate your potential, and expose the magnificence that is already inside you. This book includes true stories of actual psychic events and tips and techniques for starting your intuitive journey.

978-0-7387-4028-7, 336 pp., 5.19 x 8   **$16.99**

365 WAYS
to
DEVELOP
your
PSYCHIC ABILITY
Simple Tools to
Increase Your Intuition
& Clairvoyance
ALEXANDRA CHAURAN

365 Ways to Develop Your Psychic Ability
Simple Tools to Increase Your Intuition & Clairvoyance
Alexandra Chauran

Go from intuitive but clueless to psychic mastery in a year! *365 Ways to Develop Your Psychic Ability* is a daily study guide and course to develop your psychic abilities. Become Alexandra Chauran's psychic apprentice as you learn meditation, trance techniques, divination, and how to perform readings.

Rather than inundating the complete beginner with information, the reader is encouraged to work through the book at her own pace, day by day, absorbing the information and stretching those psychic muscles. Beginning with simple observation skills and moving forward to complex trance and divination techniques, the reader is slowly guided to mastery.

978-0-7387-3930-4, 360 pp., 5 x 7   **$17.99**

To order, call 1-877-NEW-WRLD or visit llewellyn.com
Prices subject to change without notice